CHRISTINE JORDIS was responsible for English literature at the British Council for twelve years and is now the English-language fiction editor at the French publishing house Gallimard. *Gens de la Tamise*, a panoramic study of the twentieth-century British novel, won the Prix Médicis.

CHRISTINE JORDIS

BALI, JAVA, IN MY DREAMS

Illustrated by Sacha Jordis
Maps by Emily Hare Faccini
Translated from the French
by George Bland

THE HARVILL PRESS
LONDON

Published by The Harvill Press 2002

2 4 6 8 10 9 7 5 3 1

Originally published in France by Éditions du Rocher, 2001, as *Bali, Java, en rêvant*

First published in Great Britain in 2002 by
The Harvill Press
Random House, 20 Vauxhall Bridge Road,
London SW1V 2SA

Random House Australia (Pty) Limited
20 Alfred Street, Milsons Point, Sydney,
New South Wales 2061, Australia

Random House New Zealand Limited
18 Poland Road, Glenfield,
Auckland 10, New Zealand

Random House South Africa (Pty) Limited
Endulini, 5A Jubilee Road, Parktown 2193, South Africa

The Random House Group Limited Reg. No. 954009
www.randomhouse.co.uk

A CIP catalogue record for this book
is available from the British Library

ISBN 1 860 46995 7

Typeset by Palimpsest Book Production Limited,
Polmont, Stirlingshire

Printed and bound in Great Britain by
Biddles Ltd, Guildford & Kings Lynn

To Charles and Maria, thanks to whom
I discovered Indonesia

To Sacha

ACKNOWLEDGEMENTS

I should like to thank Jean-Pascal Elbaz, Director of the Centre culturel français at Yogyakarta and a resident Indonesia for ten years, for our long discussions and for his advice on a reading list.

"Nothing, be it ever so small or commonplace, but is inhabited by the spirit and the gods!"

Hölderlin

TABLE OF CONTENTS

JAKARTA

BALI

JAVA

JAKARTA

Cambodia

Vietnam

Brunei

Malaysia

Singapore

South
China
Sea

Sumatra

Kalimantan
(Borneo)

Indian Ocean

JAVA

INDO

Lombok

Sumbava

BALI

1000m

DEPARTURE

WE WERE NOT OLD INDONESIA HANDS, NOT REALLY, BUT WE liked to imagine we were. Two trips in a matter of months, four times seventeen hours in the air, to be precise: this, for people who did not as a rule stray far from home, represented something more than a casual interest – it was the start of a passion.

We found ourselves wanting to discover more: no longer simply to explore our same two islands, Bali and Java, but to settle there, take up residence for a while – or rather to let the islands take up residence in us and let ourselves be invaded by "the spirit of the place". One day we set up house in Bali, renting an isolated villa perched high on the slopes of a volcano, Mount Batur, not far from the crater or from the village,

Kintamani. Thus did we find ourselves living in the depths of the jungle and most of the time – for we still had only a vague acquaintance with the island's peculiar climate – right in the thick of inky-black rain clouds that galloped and tumbled in a dramatic sky. They served to soften shapes and colours. In the distance, coconut palms, light pencil-strokes on the misty grey. In the evenings, the electricity network, overloaded as it tends to be in the villages of Asia, afforded us only a feeble, half-hearted glimmer of light, indeed sometimes even this tenuous illumination gave out altogether, leaving us plunged for hours on end, and sometimes until morning, in a darkness that resounded with cries and calls. Seen in the green glow of the safety lamp, the single room of our home – it had no ceiling and the roof reared up into the darkness – assumed the spectral air of a Gothic hall. From outside, beyond the wide opening, we could hear the rain dropping on the leaves and the frogs conducting solemn discussions.

Insects and frogs escaping this deluge would come and visit us, great big hairy spiders too, inoffensive creatures that darted off at the smallest movement and, right up against the bamboos at the apex of the roof, where the gloom was thickest, little fire-flies who flashed their capricious lanterns in the darkness.

Whole days were spent like this, hemmed in by the thickness of the vegetation, days when we did not see a soul other than our Balinese neighbours – days spent listening, dreaming, observing, recording.

During the twentieth century, going on a journey was more or less a political act, to go and see what was happening "on the ground", to take scrupulous notes, to come home and bear witness: Stalin's Soviet Union, where our best writers disembarked with optimism; then China, Utopia for our intellectual shock troops, a place where young volunteers went off to work in sausage factories; and, needless to say, Cuba . . . The outcome of these journeys were edifying reports, the authors acceding to the role of authentic witnesses to History. "The Orient", however, which was readily labelled a land of mirages, was the province of visionaries and dreamers of every hue. It was embedded in the leisurely explorations of the nineteenth century: Flaubert, Nerval, Loti, Rimbaud seeking "otherness", Conrad and Stevenson gravitating towards the South Seas, or Melville off to conquer a territory that is in effect the world of the spirit. "Off towards the setting sun," writes Jules Renard in his *Journal*, "beyond our horizons it seems that the world of chimera begins, parched lands, the Land of Fire, lands that project us straight into the empire of dreams . . ." Everything, that is, other than "our poor pathetic little world". "The Orient": the term belongs to an age when writers had nothing better to do than risk their lives on the ocean, march across the desert, sally into the tropics – forever setting forth, to dream, to love, to travel, to write, actions that all had a fair amount in common.

More recently, there was of course Michaux, and others of

minor celebrity, but I had none of these travellers' writings in mind when I left for Asia that first time. All I did was pay a visit to a relative who worked in Jakarta. The books came later, the guidebooks and studies likewise, and the need to return.

Sometimes in the course of the day names would come to mind, the very sound of which transported us: Java, Borneo, Sumatra, Sulawesi, Irian Jaya, Flores, Sumba, Sumbawa . . . Or else it was the heroes whose legends are treasured in these parts and who give their names to every street in Jakarta: Gajah Mada, Diponegoro, Sudirman, Hayam Wuruk, Falatehan, the painter Radén Saléh . . . I would repeat them like Proust poring over his railway timetables. Java is only a little further than Venice. Those names gave me back the wide-blue yonder, with its poetry, paradise lands for one's recollection. As for Sacha, whose vocation is to draw and paint picture-story books for children, he would recreate the images on his paper – those Indonesian pictures that are etched into the soul with all the sharpness of silhouettes traced out in Indian ink or the shadows projected on a screen of the *wayang kulit* (loosely translated as "shadow theatre").

ARRIVAL IN JAKARTA

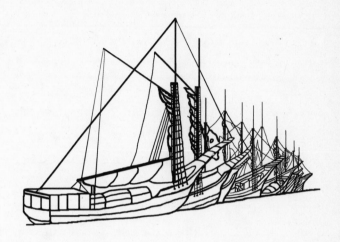

SEEN FROM THE PLANE, DURING THE RAINY SEASON – IT WAS
February – a tropical country offers a surprising range of grey
tones under a blanket of long, low, trailing clouds. From time
to time, especially in the evening but sometimes in the afternoon, these clouds swell, darken and burst, and the rain comes
pelting down on the trees, piercing the palm-thatched roofs, and
on the sea which it subdues and muffles. No sound is heard
save for the heavy, continuous stream of falling water.

The approaches to Jakarta are lined with a whole forest of
corrugated iron shacks that crowd the banks of a muddy river.
These shacks are leprous, rusty, patched together, disjointed,
knocked up all higgledy-piggledy, a fantastic patchwork of

9

ill-assorted bits and pieces with balconies all askew; only inter-
minable garlands of washing hung from the grey façades embellish them. These are the living quarters of those sorry heirs of the
nonconformist travellers, the nomads and vagabonds who once
enjoyed such prestige, *satrya lelara* playing truant as they searched
for enlightenment. Nowadays their place has been taken by the
starveling *gelandangan*, who come and press their faces to the
car windows as they pluck their guitars or spin their rattles.

Still dazed from seventeen hours' travel, enveloped in the
humid heat which, more than the passage of hours, signals the
transit into a new hemisphere, we roll gently towards the city
in a concert of car horns. Streets and more streets: a sequence
of stalls and vacant lots, buildings being torn down, and others
more recently built whose walls are already flaking and have
about them an unfinished air – the sorry sight of bare concrete
glimpsed through immense publicity hoardings.

No sign of a centre, an unpredictable, irregular filigree of
streets and lanes. A far cry from those perfect microcosms that
by their exact geometry suggested a celestial order and assigned
to each and everything a place in a grand design: the Javanese
city as once upon a time it was conceived and, occasionally,
preserved. Here, though, economic evolution and the thrust of
the skyscraper have clouded the conceptual order.

Suddenly night has fallen, the lights go on inside the booths,
shining on the vendors behind their pyramids of fruit. Schoolgirls
in their white overalls, squatting on benches and pressed close

together like birds on a perch, wait for the overloaded buses that pass in a cloud of smoke and threaten to fall to pieces at each stop. The ugliness has vanished.

The dream sparked by the very word "departure", however, or the term "long-distance voyage" – to launch out or to cast off, to eschew the "banal breezes" – this dream came to me not in the feverish moment of catching the plane, but the following day, on the quayside at Sunda Kelapa, the last port in the world, so the Javanese guidebook asserts, that is home to a fleet of mechant sailing ships.

At Sunda Kelapa, where the schooners carrying timber from Sumatra and Kalimantan drop anchor, one thinks of that sea-rover Melville, en route for Polynesia, where Segalen was to settle some fifty years later, convinced as he was that a person never grasps "the reality of that which is the Other"; one thinks of Stevenson setting sail for the South Seas, where he would die still dreaming of the ideal community he was going to found there. Or of Conrad, wounded at sea by a sliver from a spar, being put ashore in Java and hospitalised in Singapore, then deciding that, rather than return to stifling England, he would sign on as first mate on *Vidar*, a steamer of three hundred tons, and draw alongside the islands of the Malay archipelago. Here he was to meet Olmeijer, or Almayer, a highly romantic figure; only later would he sail upstream into the interior of Borneo, known today as Kalimantan. "The universe once more before us; our quest, as wide." (Melville again.)

The *Vidar* sailed from Singapore through the Straits of Karimata, which linked the South China Sea with the Java Sea. She would put in at Banjarmasin and Poulo-Laut on the south coast of Borneo, then cross the Makassar Strait, heading for Donggala, on the west coast of the Celebes, also known as Sulawesi, where they worship the dead. Expatriate Dutchmen, questionable traders, charterers who were little better than pirates, Arab and Chinese merchants, such were the folk whose paths Conrad crossed in those years. At this point, "the agony of fading youth" beset him and drove him off in search of new horizons.

Large barques with flared hulls painted in bright colours lie in rows by the quayside, mast to mast, in a unique formation that extends to the open sea. One behind the other, the high prows stand out against the sky, tracing what looks like a single, peremptory sign. The boats are connected to the jetty by plain joists laid down at unlikely angles. Some men carrying heavy teak planks walk barefoot, gingerly at first, then in a sort of gliding dance once they are on terra firma.

This activity is ceaseless. I screw up my eyes in the rain as I watch the women, clad in sarongs, coming to bring their menfolk their lunch, and the faces of these acrobatic porters when they address the women; they are dressed in rags, with turbaned heads and expressionless faces, reminiscent of the pirates of yore. Such gang leaders, deaing in weapons or in slaves, and running amok armed with their krises, ruled the waves from the eighteenth century onwards. They are straight out of the pages of

Conrad or Emilio Salgari, a writer of lesser reputation, a great dreamer in the face of Eternity; he was born in Verona in 1862 and, like Conrad, had the desire to become a sailor and move the seven seas, even though in practice he never sailed beyond the Adriatic. He lived a rich fantasy-life, between India and Borneo, in his many books only to die, his dream exhausted, by his own hand in Turin in 1911.

Lying under tarpaulins atop the woodpiles, more pirates reclined and laughed. The air was fragrant with a fresh, piquant smell – teak and rain, which in time became the very smell of Java to me.

Sunda Kelapa is close to the Chinese town. We had been paddling about in the murky water and the garbage, surrounded by the ghastly flood of two-wheeled conveyances, when at last a taxi appeared. It was still raining. We climbed in and gave my brother's address – not all that central, truth told – for we were to stay with him. How long did it take us to realise that the driver – a young man with wild eyes and a drooping moustache, who was given to sonorous burps, maybe to boost his morale – had no notion of where he was going? He kept moving, that was all. Besides, in which language could he have confessed his ignorance? The half-hours passed, the traffic jams gradually lost their charm, the same streets slid past the misted-up windows. The evening, then the night could be spent this way, just moving, moving and getting nowhere, moving along with so many others in this *perpetuum mobile*. For fear of losing face

– quite unthinkable in Indonesia – a taxi driver, as we were to discover a little too late, will never admit that he does not recognise the specified destination; he will instead await some sign from heaven (trust in divine intervention), or a flash of recollection in the white person seated behind him (a baseless trust in the tourist's omnipotence) and continue to drive, which is, of course, his proper task. Our driver, receiving no help from these sources but aware of our growing impatience, resigned himself to enquiring of passers-by and then, eventually – in a mute admission of defeat – to stopping the meter. We were well and truly lost in Jakarta.

Visiting the city's historical museum, on what is today known as Taman Fatahillah Square; looking at the heavy, pompous furniture favoured by the Dutch settlers; contemplating the official portraits of governors stiff with the sense of their own importance and infallibility, crammed into costumes that, given the ambient temperature, demanded an elevated sense of their status (if not a degree of heroism) – all this made it easy to imagine Jakarta's history. Jan Pieterzoon Coen, a young Dutch chief accountant with a taste for order, profit and numbers, and who counts among the many criminals applauded by history, had the town completely razed, then in 1619 built a new city, properly ordered this time, on the model of Amsterdam, with canals and swing bridges, docks and warehouses, barracks and central square: this was Batavia, rechristened Jakarta in 1942 after some three hundred years of Dutch occupation.

What these features suggest is corroborated in the guide's stories, horror tales linked to the colonisation, as witness here and there some object which is pointed out to one in passing, like a sword used to behead the condemned prisoners, on this very square in front of the museum, which was formerly a law court and prison but also served as the governor's palace – they had only to open their windows to watch the execution.

Rough-and-ready methods (neither courthouse nor prison) sufficed to execute the Chinese merchants in 1740, for their prosperity and influence disturbed the Dutch as much as it did the Javanese. Ten thousand Chinese were slaughtered, the first of a long series of massacres. The government regrouped the survivors and banished them beyond the city walls, rehousing them in what is now the Glodok quarter. For good measure they deprived them of a number of privileges that had contributed to their power and unpopularity, like tax-gathering and controlling the markets. No-one liked the Chinese any better, but from this point the Dutch East India Company enjoyed exclusive command of the north coast of Java.

We took a walk in Glodok. Not a sign of Chinese characters, not a panel, not an inscription. It is only recently that the New Year celebrations, with dragons, fireworks, masks and smoke signals, have again been permitted. Before that, both the language and the festivals were banned. Furthermore they had to choose an Indonesian name, forsaking the recognizable trisyllabic *xing-ming*. What did Suharto want: to disguise the characters that most distinguished a population suffering from Javanese hostility, or simply to stamp out an identity that had been preserved with great tenacity? Was it harassment or the urge towards integration? As a consequence, you must peer deep inside the dark shops to believe that you have penetrated into Chinatown, which is an inextricable labyrinth with pagoda-style roofs, narrow gabled houses ("the Amsterdam of the South"), antiquated colonial buildings and, along the canals with their filthy water bobbing with empty bottles, dented tins, plastic bags and all manner of junk, age-old warehouses forever on the point of collapse. This part of town has taken its revenge on the Nordic order that threatened it, replacing it with a principle of anarchy that works well enough: with lanes turning into alleyways, booths into markets. This area constantly lures the visitor onwards towards a non-existent centre, confusing him, spinning him in circles, rolling him like a beach pebble, submerging him in strange impressions and exhalations, leaving him defenceless and deprived of landmarks, shorn of all judgement and ability to make comparisons – consigned, in a word, to a different set of rules.

The sweet, fetid smell of rotting, coming in waves, submerges that of exhaust fumes. The aroma of spices and flowers is a discreet counterpoint. A complete mélange . . .

It is in one of these streets strewn with garbage and clogged with cars and trishaws (or *bajaj*) that the temple of Dharma Jaya, with its strange portico, is located. At first glance the dragons painted in garish colours suggest a gypsy fair rather than a shrine – one dating back, moreover, to 1652. No doubt about it, though: once across the austere little inner courtyard and over the temple threshold, we find ourselves enveloped in a sultry semi-darkness lit by hundreds of tiny flames from the oil lamps, in a forest of smoking joss sticks stuck in high stands. The atmosphere is so thick, we can barely make out the dozens of gods and goddesses smiling in their niches; our eyes smart as we advance through a cloud of smoke. Grouped by families in small rooms like so many chapels, the statues are draped in heavy ceremonial mantles that make Spain's Blessed Virgins look soberly dressed in comparison; a few pilgrims seeking shade and refuge from the clamour of the street worship them. An improvised guide shows us the god who receives the most solicitations, the one before whom tourists and canned-food merchants bow: the god of money.

Not far from there, proving that the cults blend or coexist without showing the smallest resemblance in the way they are expressed, the Portuguese church of Gereya Sion is the very model of Protestant austerity. It is said that the Dutch built it in 1790 for the descendants of the Indian slaves brought in by the Portuguese merchants. They would come into this big, bare white building, which is supported on six massive pillars, and maybe they found some comfort in the opulence of the pulpit set in the dead centre of the church, behind the high altar, with its twisted baroque columns covered in the gilded volutes of a painted vine. An unexpected luxuriousness that is complemented by the huge chandeliers with the long gentle curves of their branches.

To cover the short distance from the temple to the church we took a trishaw, little suspecting the ordeal we were imposing on ourselves. These vehicles, which today have replaced the *becak*, carry their tightly packed cargo of passengers for a few rupees. There is prestige in mechanisation and power in the motor, and these have replaced the stride of women bearing their heavy burden of merchandise on their heads. Ignition requires the use of a piece of string, rather reminiscent of old-time outboard motors, but the racket is more akin to that of an aircraft taking off, not that this adds much to the general noise-level and the incessant blast of car horns. Once inside the *bajaj* there is no chance of moving anymore than the vehicle itself, hemmed in as it is by other vehicles equally stalled; the corrugated iron panels shudder, the exhaust fumes escape in eddies making a screen evenly distributed in the atmosphere. Prisoners in the metal walls heated by a white-hot sun, we slowly suffocate, like the English colonel played by Alec Guinness in *The Bridge on the River Kwai* whom the Japanese incarcerate in a cell not unlike our own in order to break him. From time to time we catch glimpses of the street, half-veiled by the grey miasma of pollution, of broad-cheeked faces, goods being unloaded in bails, shop doorways where a merchant sits enthroned – a kaleidoscopic vision of a typical day in Asia.

JAVA MAN

AT AN INTERSECTION IN JAKARTA, STANDING LIKE A GIANT
exclamation mark in the thick of the maddening traffic, a statue
of Youth conjures up the heyday of socialist realism and Soviet
influence: a broad-featured native Javanese, chest swelling over
a heroic ripple of muscles, bears at arm's length a circular dish
on which burns the flame of Energy – the Jakartans, with blithe
disrespect, have christened the object "pizza pie".

We will again encounter this victorious human being nearby,
this time at the moment of his birth, reduced to a few celebrated bones displayed in a glass case. The National Museum
of Java is a small building in classical style, looking somewhat
the worse for wear even if it houses the evidence of a crucial
discovery concerning the human race – in the modest shape of

a cranial cap (not even a full skull) and a femur deformed by disease. Before East Africa stole its thunder with tools dating back two and a half million years, Java was believed to be the cradle of humanity; in any event, the discovery of Java Man confirmed the "missing link" hypothesis, the irrefutable proof that the ape is the ancestor of the human.

Eugène Dubois, a Dutch anatomy professor who had the misfortune of engaging in research shortly after the publication of Darwin's *Origin of Species*, had an *idée fixe* that was to cause him considerable grief. He was fascinated with Neanderthal Man and the theory of evolution. After much thought he concluded that Darwin's famous "missing link" was to be found in Sumatra, where so many orang-utans had evolved. (Today, decimated by fires and deforestation, the orang-utans have left many orphans; these are sheltered in a private zoo at Jakarta by an elderly German lady of the aristocracy – no doubt regarding them as close cousins, she has devoted her life to them.) Lacking the necessary means to mount an expedition, Dubois resigned from the teaching profession and enlisted as doctor in the Dutch East Indian army. He hoped thus to come close to the place of his dreams. He was indeed posted to Sumatra but in no time he caught "the fevers". Fate did not seem to be on his side, but on this occasion she smiled on him: once transferred to Java, he had ample leisure to explore the region of Solo and its fossil deposits. The Dutch authorities even gave him a few convicts to lend a hand with his excavations.

This was the era, though, when the trade in aphrodisiacs was flourishing, especially with China. These wonder drugs that the Chinese merchants sought for their price in gold were derived from finely ground bones. The convicts, who lacked Dubois' own high regard for fossils, saw in the heaps of bones entrusted to them a miraculous opportunity to strike it rich: the chances are that Java Man, surviving in but three fragments, as well as many others of his tribe, was ground up and ingested in powder form by lovelorn Chinamen, contributing in the process to the enrichment of Java's convicts.

In 1891, however, Dubois' perseverance was rewarded: he dug up three fragments of human skeleton – the remains of which he baptised *Pithecanthropus erectus*, the "missing link" between Man and Ape. His long-standing intuition was coming true, the end of the dream was in sight. Alas, this was making no allowances for the Church and contemporary society, which proclaimed that Man was conceived in the image and likeness of God and could not in logic be descended from the ape. They could not rest until they had sent Java Man packing, and his inventor with him. And they succeeded by way of accusations, attacks and all manner of campaigns. Dubois pressed ahead with his work for a while, then wearily threw up palaeontology for good.

Thus concluded the adventure of Eugène Dubois, that compulsive dreamer whose failure was attributable to the ruthless conceit of the era. He is one of those Utopians, scholars, rebels and artists, the whole tribe of outsiders, inventors at odds with society, who were drawn to the island of Java to the point of inscribing their fate on it, drawn to the entire Indonesian archipelago where no dream, no vaporous imaginings, however odd, no chimera, no phantasm, however delirious, seemed impossible or even surprising.

But that was not the end of the story. In 1921, further excavations, this time at Peking, finally vindicated Dubois. They resurrected the *Homo erectus* of Java, who appeared at Sanginan, close to the banks of the Bengawan Solo River, some one and a half million years ago and who fits, as the labels in the National Museum confirm, between *Homo habilis* and the archaic *Homo sapiens*.

It is important to bear in mind that Java Man knew no language but communicated by sounds, lived in caves and especially – of no small importance, it seems to me – he was the first to discover the use of fire.

Beneath the top of the skull, which looks like a cap, the piece of jawbone and the femur, we read: "A study of the bones and teeth attests deformity, murder, wounds, inadequate diet – too rich in sulphur (plentiful in volcanic soil) – premature death, etc."

BALI

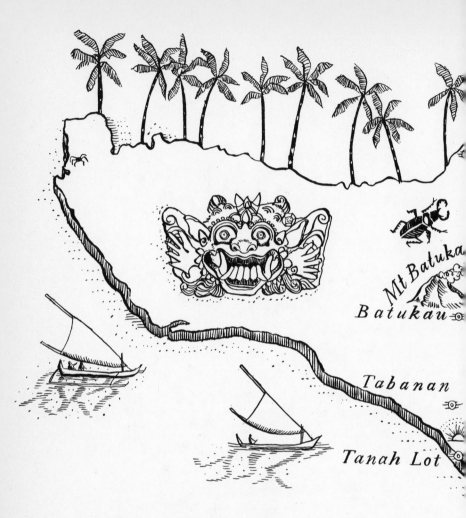

Mt Batuka

Batukau

Tabanan

Tanah Lot

BALI

30m

DENPASAR

AT DENPASAR AIRPORT WE ARE GREETED BY THE SIGHT OF temples with winged portals, all red and fretted, as Balinese in elegant rose or green sarongs, their foreheads covered in bandanas, wait around and smile. A little of the island's mysterious allure thus displays itself – in the white flash of a smile addressed to life, to the sun or the gods rather than to the visitor, who is less a nuisance than an irrelevance. (In any case, the visitor is quickly sent on his way in accordance with his appearance or calling, be it to Kuta for the surf, to Sanur where the sea is calmer, or to Ubud, the New Age town, these being the three tourist destinations on Bali.) Among them slips a ghost left over from the 1970s, a scrawny hippie, long hair loose over his shoulders, his chest covered in tattoos, a concession to fashion; like a disembodied shadow he threads his way through the little crowd without exciting interest.

On the squares of Denpasar, the capital, we see no representations of war leaders or renowned statesmen, not like in our own distant Hexagon where they are accorded an inexplicable pride of place – their effigies discreetly await the passer-by under the shade of a tree, their bearing military, arms stiff, chin raised, foot extended as though meaning to step out. Instead, there are scenes from the *Mahabharata*, a far cry from the greenish modesty of these statues.

Already at the first crossroads we come to a gigantic monument made of snowy-white plastic and designed with a frenetic expressionism. It introduces myth and drama into the very heart of the explosive, traffic-flooded twentieth century. A ballet of twirling figures, horses pawing the ground, rearing up, neighing, manes streaming, and bug-eyed archers. Gatukaca, son of Bima – the second of the five Pandawa brothers – is grappling with Karna, the adversary of the great Arjuna, who is also a Pandawa. At this crucial moment the magic arrow has not yet pierced him, the one that was to win victory for the enemy, the Kurawa brothers, in slaying Arjuna. The traffic flows round the frenzied sculpture without managing to reduce its movement. The *Mahabharata*, a complete book, poem, epic, written in Sanskrit at the beginning of our era and fifteen times longer than the Bible, continues to spread its flood of tales in grottoes and temples, in the smallest crevices of the island and of the minds of its inhabitants, where only that other great Indian epic, the *Ramayana*, can compete. In the course of the festivals and rituals, which are numerous, in the middle of towns, villages, squares (*alunalun*) and palaces, scenes from it are performed, danced, relived, always the same ones, each time subtly transformed (the *Mahabharata* is the book that says everything). Today, however, the tendency is to favour the *Ramayana*, which dramatises the concerted efforts of a society striving for a common goal: to uproot evil. With its fratricidal struggles in the bosom of a single community, the *Mahabharata* has become altogether too sensitive a contemporary issue.

Zigzagging between the stalls and the palm trees, the road, filled with potholes from the rains, makes its way to the sea. A sharp bend brings us in sight of the hotel, or rather of its gateway and its stone guardians, two little demons in tattered sarongs; the rest of the building is screened by a dark thickness of foliage. In the middle of the path a very ancient woman, tiny as a child and richly ornamented, kneels between the puddles and peacefully makes her offering of flowers to some invisible goddess.

The brochures assure us that the island is the archetype of beauty, while the best regarded sociologists claim that we must imagine it as "a sort of aesthetic Arcadia". The meeting place of aesthetes and artists, the focal point for the cream of the international set: the 1920s and 1930s, the era of Walter Spies, Rudolf Bonnet, Vicki Baum and Michel Covarrubias . . .

The chance to discover heaven at a knock-down price – since 1970, the start of mass tourism . . .

In the nineteenth century, the bell had a somewhat different sound: the opium habit, decadence, civil wars, suttee for widows, the slave trade, and furthermore, in the mountains, instead of the famous Balinese breasts, the most horrible goitres were "all too common a sight". "There is scarcely a woman who is not misshapen by these excrescences," Élisée Reclus writes in Volume XIV of his *Nouvelle Géographie universelle*.

Quite possibly. Between out-and-out censure and the cut-and-dried image of a suckers' paradise, it's not for me to choose. In any case, it's common to pronounce the word "beauty", like that of "paradise", with a touch of disdain towards those who are dupes of opinions that are too widespread and therefore suspect, or towards those who go by outward appearances only.

As for me, I prefer to believe in these outward appearances: like the legend that a person creates around him (and which is, according to Oscar Wilde, more important than what a man actually does), appearances often reveal what is truest about ourselves: not so much what we are in our humdrum moments as what we strive to be, the salient point of our desires. Forever intent on revealing what lies behind the scenes – the fear (*lek*, which would be the equivalent to our stage fright) or the flaw (often mistaken for the truth) that lies behind the façade – the scholars have believed themselves capable of identifying in every instant of a Balinese person's life the fear of losing face. But why should such a fear be more real, or deeper, than the Balinese concern for beauty (beauty as a gift charged with re-establishing order in the world)?

It is true that the islanders are at grips with Nature in so lively, indeed violent and unpredictable a form, with its pronounced taste for exaggeration and melodrama, that they are constantly on their guard, well recognising that this all-powerful Nature must be respected, but never trusted. Let their attention be distracted for one moment and Nature regains the upper hand, recovering lost ground, restoring the eternal law of excess precisely where, by dint of care and prudence, they had arrived at an equal distribution.

And so it is that a faultless regulation governs their existence at the same time, so they hope, as the cosmos in which it is inscribed. But this rapport with nature, how do we know they find it burdensome? The boundlessness of natural forces is the perspective in which they live. They must constantly measure themselves against the sea, the clouds, the volcanoes; and it is this dialogue with the unlimited that orientates their life, that gives it breadth and meaning.

He will be a cunning one who can slip behind the smile of a Balinese and say whether this smile, this ready, spontaneous, friendly smile conceals a weariness at submitting to the complex rituals of daily living or, on the contrary, a satisfaction at belonging to a world in which his place and his role are so well defined. It is nonetheless worth noting in passing that such codes are endemic in the entire community's consciousness, practised from generation to generation, and by now second nature.

The island is the abode of sorcerers, demons and gods. It is an emerald drawn from the ocean depths that rests on the broad back of a tortoise. According to the legend: "While meditating, Antaboga, the serpent of the world, created Bedawang the tortoise on which rest two intertwined serpents, who are the foundation of the universe."

The gods dwell on the mountain tops while the demons hide in the hollows and caves. Halfway up, partaking of the two worlds, the air and the sea, there is the middle part reserved for humans, a separation into three levels that orders everything down to the last inch, a hierarchy conforming to an overall cosmic plan: the architecture of the houses and villages, the pavilions and temples, and of the human body. Djero Gedé Metjaling, the giant with the pointed teeth who lives on the barren island of Nusa Penida, governs the coastal strip; he is an evil spirit, a frontiersman, subject to the pernicious winds that blow on the crossroads, intersections, on the forests and beaches. So the Balinese do not gaze over the sea surrounding them and from which their invaders came, but up to the summits, to the volcanoes that dominate their island, to the Gunung Agung, which is the highest and the most sacred.

OF DEMONS AND GODS

In order to hold on to the moments of solitude which are so necessary, I had gone to wander in the area surrounding our hotel. I had turned my back on the main street where the motorcycles were still passing in the infernal heat. Even so, it was almost night. Little grocers' stalls, the *warung*, their entire fronts open to the street, offered their bric-a-brac, bottles, jars, tins, bags and bulging sacks and, high up in a corner, the blurred, quivering picture from the small television screens that nobody thought to watch. Another turning and suddenly the lights, along with the shops, had disappeared.

It is not surprising that the entire island – from the day when it first emerged from the sea, it may be confidently affirmed –

is dedicated to magic. One has only to turn off a main thoroughfare and one feels this magic at work, with no need for any outside intervention, devilish artifice or secret ceremony. Perhaps it is all down to the density of the night, or to the exuberance of outsized vegetation that at this very moment crouches in the darkness, or to the enveloping heat, palpable and immediate as an invisible presence. Silent paths, like a labyrinth buried beneath the plants. A closed door decorated with an interlacing of symbols and over-elaborate carvings, which guards the mystery of a garden whose splendour is to be imagined just from the scent of the flowers fallen on to the pathway – white, waxy petals of a large frangipani. Here and there a glimmer of light, a halo in the thick darkness, indicates a human presence: and yet not a sound. On the threshold of her house a woman squats, accomplishing the slow, precise gestures of the rite of offering.

When it comes to offerings, the island is spoilt for choice. There is not an hour of the day, not a moment in human life, not a date in the calendar that does not have its prescriptive right to prayers and libations. The air is so a-buzz with demons and spirits hell-bent on fighting each other that human beings have their work cut out to contain all these restless presences. In the thick of the battle humanity strives to re-establish an equilibrium, calming the one side and thanking the other. Spiritual harmony is in constant need of reconquering, peace forever needs restoring between the conflicting factions of negative and positive forces that are unleashed at the drop of a hat: birth, menstruation, a death in the village, a crime or merely a petty theft, every occasion is good for interfering in the lives of the inhabitants and troubling the magic harmony that they had obtained by virtue of gifts.

And that is only the evil spirits, those troublemakers who sow discord: it is up to humans to keep them down. Above these pests of limited power, the gods lead their own lives and work to a vastly superior agenda, since with them it is a matter of the very life of the cosmos. Beyond the ripples of minor disputes, their activities link up and complement one other, creation and destruction are all enmeshed, which is not to say that the gods have no interest in human transactions or that humanity is not required to conciliate them – and their spouses, come to that, for they can play an even more pernicious role, like Durga, the discarded wife of Shiva, who reigns over death and over those who deal in it.

Destruction, incarnate in Shiva,[1] to which the island devotes a particular cult, is by no means a purely negative force but the precondition for renewal, the obligatory stage on the way to the continual rebirth of the world; therefore one cannot take too much issue with the great upheavals that the god in his wisdom inflicts – he is the trusty ally of Vishnu, the preserver of life. The two of them together, under the benevolent eye of Brahma, assure the proper ordering of the universe.

---

[1] The Hindu trinity comprises Brahma, Vishnu and Shiva, adapted to meet the needs of local cults.

Rangda, the witch, the bloodthirsty widow who devours children, a female version of Saturn or Cronos, who ate his own children, is an old woman with pendulous breasts, entirely covered in a tangled mass of white hair from which nothing protrudes but her bulging eyes and menacing fangs. In the legend her adversary, Bharada, slays her in her monstrous shape then restores her to life and gives her a human shape so that she might expiate her crimes, then he slays her all over again. But in staged representations there is no execution: it is useless to slay Rangda, the incarnation of night and death, of evil and envy; a person is possessed just as a scorpion stings or a bride is faithful. The Plan of the World is so devised that it must reckon with evil and even handle it with kid gloves. No point hoping to defeat it. Rather than deny its existence or imagine that, with greater knowledge, they might get the better of it on the next occasion ("never again" is the cry of the simple-minded), the Balinese have the wisdom to recognise its might, its ever-renewed virulence. To the negative powers operating in the universe, to those involved in the works of death – hatred, bitterness, greed, jealousy and similar ugly urges that arrive all too frequently to torment humans – they have consecrated temples where they repair once a year in great pomp, hoping to neutralise the demons who keep us company or hold us in thrall. In the north of the island, where the temples are black and constructed in a softer stone, worked over-elaborately, one of the most funereal buildings, the Pura Dalem at Singaraya, has been dedicated to Rangda, the spirit of evil. The death's head, garlanded with the weeds that have invaded the façades, carved in hundreds of copies, glares at the visitor with hungry eyes. In the empty noonday sky, beneath a murderous sun, the seething mass of these grimacing heads, half-emerging with a fierce grin from the darkness of the stone, charges the place with a subtle presence.

The only recourse is to exert some influence upon the alternation of the currents that flow and ebb, advance then retreat like great tides, to appease the spirits by thwarting the evil with a counterweight of harmony and beauty: flowers, fruit, leaves and clusters, woven baskets and trays, pyramids of dark colours in which the bright red of the hibiscus sings out loud, evanescent works of art patiently elaborated and dismantled the same day. Long hours are spent making these offerings before they may be admired swaying gently on the heads of the women, cunning structures that vie with each other for craftsmanship; then they are all consumed in the temple feasts. In this way the world is re-established after tottering an instant on its foundations; north, south, east and west are brought into line after a spell behaving like urchins playing tag.

And then there is the Barong, Djero Gedé, "king of the jungle", embodiment of the sun and the daylight, even though he too is a monster. He rehearses the eternal drama of this struggle in the course of trance-like rituals; with his prancing and his unbridled leaps, by his clownish vitality and buffoonery, he exorcises fear and even death, which retreats while the dancers spin like tops or roll in the dust, pressing with all their might on the krises that they have pointed against their chests.

Better to take precautions and forestall evils rather than cure them: the dances, rituals, anniversaries and other sacred feasts that impel all the villagers in single file towards the temples do not always preserve the ideal harmony. A few moments of distraction and chaos resumes its sway, like the savage jungle invading an area conquered by hard labour. It is therefore necessary to include many small private celebrations to counter the neighbour's little schemes or the activities of so-called natural forces. Three grains of rice deposited on a scrap of banana leaf on the threshold of a house, a few flower petals in a woven platter on the wall of a bridge across a ravine. Three derisory grains of rice, like Tom Thumb's pebbles, like a fragile talisman to confront the abundance of boulders and giant tree roots.

We came upon such an offering one day on the mossy parapet of an old bridge at Tjampuhan, near Ubud. From the road on a precipice we noticed below us deep in the heart of the tropical forest the brown roofs and ochred stones of a riverside temple. Following the river we reached the bottom of the ravine, close to the temple. Above the little basket that had been so carefully constructed, the trees, for which no void, no impossibility exists, had decided to undertake a massive demonstration of their power. A giant banyan tree, which blocked the sky and hid the daylight from us, plunged its roots which were as thick as ropes into the thirty-metre-deep abyss that it overhung. The angle of attachment to the side of the chasm, the dense rain of colossal roots, the dizzying height of the tree – and the daintiness of the tiny offering which was trying to conciliate . . . well, what?

Imagine an order remote from any kind of fixity, that is born from a conflict of opposites and therefore in constant need of reassertion: such an order seemed to me to hold the key to true wisdom, fully meshed in the complexity of reality. Harmony is the gift of those who have avoided the temptations of an extreme and partial view of life (something unknown in this island's philosophy), and are able to take realities of differing and even conflicting orders and *connect* them, and to perceive the general law underlying them. With their constant offerings, made impartially to good spirits and evil ones, the Balinese had grasped this lesson.

In the countryside each family has a shrine of its own and each village has not one temple but three, these ones being official and dedicated to the trinity, the first to Brahma the supreme god and arbiter, the second to Shiva the destructive force, and the third to Vishnu to whom falls the opposite task of creating; so it is that, across the island, more shrines are visible than houses.

One day as we were driving down a narrow country road at dusk – the twilight hour when shapes become indistinct – we were brought up short by a strange sight. A procession was winding along the opposite slope like a ribbon of gold; at its head went women in full ceremonial attire with offerings on trays; then came the men decked in white and in yellow silk, bearing palanquins; then came the *barong*, monstrous beast, half-lion half-dragon, symbol of life, caparisoned in gold and mirrors; lastly the musicians playing their cymbals and beating on gongs. They advanced in the uncertain glimmer of the fading twilight, all keeping pace and moved, it seemed, by the dry, monotonous rhythm of the percussion instruments. The fringed parasols waved high above their heads. To watch them progressing thus, their eyes on the distance, as if each were haunted by the selfsame dream, a fabulous caravan out of a distant Orient where the Queen of Sheba visited Solomon, one had the impression that the entire troupe – musicians, monster and dancers – was about to vanish with the remains of the day, to disappear from one moment to the next like a mirage. But no, as we watched them come towards us, they turned one by one and penetrated into the darkness of a road that led to the temple.

An image. One of those that snatches you out of yourself. That leaves you spellbound. This image was subsequently reinforced by many others, of even greater intensity, with considerable crowds and an unprecedented display of magnificence, during the ceremony of Galungen, on 2 August, which celebrates the victory of the cosmic order over chaos.

Night had fallen on my reflections and on the labyrinth of dark streets. I took the road back to the hotel. Tonight we were to make an incursion into tourist country, a million miles from the magic of the island.

SANUR

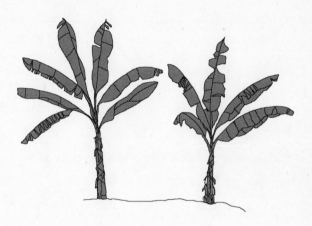

BY THE SEASIDE AT SANUR, WHERE WE ARE TAKING A NIGHT-time stroll, the great empty hotels, with their rows of chaises longues as if for the sick in an old-fashioned sanatorium, await the tourists who are sadly low in number – the political troubles have chased them away. As a concession to this invisible mass tourism, a final and vain effort at seduction addressed to some chairs, a solitary little band plays a languid mix of island tunes and American songs. Harry Belafonte and Frank Sinatra: a hybrid pair which suddenly shrinks the distances, abolishes the differences and flings us, bound hand and foot, into this impersonal hotel salon that extends from one end of the planet to the other, far from our own end of the world. The four musicians wear Hawaiian shirts; their voices dominate the solemn nocturnal song of the toads. Luckily, it takes only a very few steps to re-enter the night. Safe from the assault of international bad taste, we congratulate ourselves on the discretion of our more modest home which offers, for all distraction, nothing beyond the frail and subtly repetitive notes of the gamelan[1] early in the morning.

The next day, back from a day of touring, we go into the dining room, a sort of paddock open on every side to the darkness and the sound of the sea. The room is vast and empty. We have hardly sat down when our four musicians from the previous night appear. We keep our eyes on our plates. Without being discouraged by our visible lack of enthusiasm, they bravely strike up the same tunes as the night before. No further tourists arrive, this is a risk of the rainy season. At random, we become the heroes of the evening. We are asked to name our preferred songs. With no other clues, but informed of our nationality by the zealous waiter, the musicians are now bleating in chorus 'Frère Jacques', followed by *"J'ai gravé sur le sable son doux visage / Et j'ai pleuré, crié pour qu'elle revienne, Aline . . ."* in an Indonesian accent which might well have lent a new interest to the song had it not run beyond ten verses. Only an effort at goodwill, combined with a sense of the pathos of the situation, enabled us to hide our consternation.

That was our only tribute to tourism in Bali. The following

---

[1] A native Indonesian orchestra featuring mainly percussion instruments.

day we were to leave for the interior – Batur, Bratan, Klungkung, Ubud (where we were nonetheless to run into a few tourists), Tampaksiring . . .

AT KINTAMANI

SURROUNDED BY TREACHEROUS CURRENTS THAT LONG
protected it from invaders, and by dangerous coral reefs for
good measure, the island is dominated at the four points of the
compass by the high peaks of its volcanoes. At least two of
them, Gunung Agung and Gunung Batur, keep it on its toes.
Downpours of rain, erupting volcanoes, murderous lava flows.
The islanders know the weight to attach to racing clouds, a
darkening sky, wind that shakes the trees and a river that swells,
as also to earth that shifts, the prelude to disaster.

To counter mere nothings, the naughty pranks committed
by a lower order of devils – things like sickness and premature
death – the magic charge of energy contained in the human

body could suffice, provided, of course, that care is taken to keep it intact, which depends largely on sound spiritual and moral health. An old rajah, whose exertions had transformed him into a living electric battery, would pin his adversary to the ground with a single glance, a single discharge. It is easy to see that power of this sort has little to do with good and evil, being rather a question of harmony with the way the world turns. It is also clear that this power has two sides, recto and verso, and that it can be flipped as easily as a coin: the gods turn into demons, just as life turns to death. The converse is equally true.

As for the major catastrophes, tidal waves, earthquakes, volcanic eruptions and other whims of the cosmos, little can be done about them. Twice Gunung Batur has exploded into life. The first time, the lava buried the village of Batur and stopped at the very gates of the temple – the omen was clear, the villagers caught on at once and stayed put. The second occasion, some ten years later (what crime had they committed in the interval?), the volcano decided to destroy everything, the temple included.

At Kintamani, by the edge of the old crater, a handful of harpies – no doubt the descendants of those stubborn villagers – greet us after the long ascent, just as we're leaving our car. With flattened faces, skin drawn tight over the cheekbones, copper-coloured complexion, they are far from possessing the sunny charm of the Balinese. "Sarong, madame?" "You must have a sarong." But we are not short of sarongs. Sacha, less combative that day, finds himself belted in yellow silk in no time at all. Down below, in the plain, it was as hot as an oven. Up here, caught in the clouds that crown the volcano, we are shivering. Tugged and jostled, dogged by the crowd of vituperative hawkers, we finally reach the temple enclosure, and there the women leave us.

Across the threshold a deathly silence reigns. We are at the foot of a vast stone staircase. At the top, two great dark spectral wings overshadow us, their tips pointing skywards – two baleful shadows out of *Nosferatu* or some other Murnau film. It is the gate of the temple of Batur, revealing nothing beyond the opacity of the clouds. Wafts of rain-sodden mist tear by rapidly, occasionally hiding it from our eyes: in the midst of the yellow vapour we see nothing except for fragments of the dark silhouette.

The place is so inhospitable, the cold so penetrating that we soon leave to walk along the ridge and explore the chaotic upthrust of the volcanoes. Under the sky, as if scooped into a basket for a race of titans, rice paddies are in abundance: coconut fronds, stretches of grass-speckled water, shades of green issuing from the black lava.

Under the monstrous pressure the crater has literally exploded, digging out this amphitheatre some fifteen kilometres across, from which a second crater has emerged, this one smaller but just as aggressive and still smouldering. On the shores of the peaceful lake which half surrounds it, a surviving village harbours the Bali Aga, the island's most primeval inhabitants, who have been convinced of their own importance, and even of their invulnerability, by this favour of fate. Perhaps they are not wrong: it seems that they are the legitimate descendants of *Pithecanthropus erectus*, whose stone tools were discovered among the more recent bones of their dead. In the graveyard of Trunyan, on the far shore of Lake Batur, the Bali Aga are content to expose their dead to the wind, the sun and the rain, an archaic ritual only permitted by the strange power of a tree that happens to grow there: it spares the villagers from the disagreeable odour of putrefaction.

THE MOTHER TEMPLE

THEN WE RESUMED THE ROAD FOR BESAKIH.

The "Mother Temple", the holiest of sanctuaries, Besakih stands halfway along the sky road that is touched by the summit of Gunung Agung, the most powerful volcano on the island (as a recent eruption lethally demonstrated). The Balinese consider it to be the Navel of the World. Besakih is the favourite abode of the spirits and the dead: those who approach it do so at their own risk.

Born beneath other skies and different laws, the tourist has nothing to fear, nor anything to gain, by penetrating into the awesome precincts. His presence is neutral, indifferent, neither adding nor detracting from that which lies infinitely far beyond it. To conform with the regulations he has managed to drape a sarong round his shorts, tied the traditional belt round his expanding waist and, thus accoutred, armed with his camera, prudently wearing a hat whose soft brim almost sits on his nose, he recalls those genial monsters at the temple gates, or the popular characters in the *wayang kulit*. To the extent that he is at all conscious of the figure he cuts, he finds it difficult to blend with the austere spirit of the place – this complex of eighteen temples perched high amid the clouds. And yet, he finds it all so strange – this dream of stone so beautiful, these hundreds of crenellated towers protruding like spikes from the mountainside – that he will soon lose that self-consciousness that alienates him from both himself and his surroundings.

The villagers have dressed in their festive attire. White and gold, symbolic colours, for the men. Mauve, pink, violet, crimson, black or green for the women, who carry on their heads the great big baskets of offerings.

In one long single file of singing colours they climb at a regular pace through the heavy morning heat up the last steep kilometre separating them from the supernatural kingdom of the spirits.

Wings, wheels, carts, blackish spikes, sharpened points, accretions of lava: the temples cling to the slope, and raise their extravagant, jagged, dark profiles towards the sky. Then comes the last one of all, the highest, which is not to be approached unless with the tremor occasioned by the sacred. The temple's gateway, fixed against the massive backdrop of the mountain, is a gaping dragon's jaw opened wide on the spreading vista. In the centre stand the empty chairs (*padmasana*) of Surya, the ancient sun-god, and of Vishnu, Shiva and Brahma: no representation of the gods, only a suggested presence.

The offerings are placed on the altars. The women chatter and laugh. The gamelan prepares itself, the musicians in red sarongs and white jackets put the finishing touches to their costume. The dance is about to begin. Within a few minutes one is bewitched.

Beauty, along with all its other advantages, has this one as well: it takes us out of ourselves by surprise – occasionally a shock of surprise – and pleasure. Beauty is not a reminder, it does not speak of me – it *is*, that is all, like fullness as distinct from emptiness, like an absolute presence, self-sufficient and imperative. Free from doubt and disquiet, I can be absorbed in it, cling to it; beauty is fullness of existence, certainty that has no need to include me. And this certainty, as it engulfs me, gives me a boundless joy – a joy that perhaps also derives quite simply from the freedom of stepping outside of my customary limits (something of a prison, come to think of it), a joy that we feel with intensity when we are wrapped up in a spectacle, when we can make ourselves transparent, turn ourselves into the very faculty of watching – of merely being, with no distance or separation, just being entirely present in the thing we are observing. (A measure of intrusive vulgarity brings us back to ourselves and our petty reflexes of irritation, so that we have considerable difficulty in concentrating on the sight of a Greek temple while within its cramped confines – no problem with *that* – circulate boisterous crowds with their beer bellies, their bottom-clinging shorts and gaping T-shirts, the Western tourists in all their tactless vulgarity, the polar opposite to the norms of the East. "Beauty will be an irritant or it will be nothing," a friend said to me on returning from Florence, where he visited the Medici tombs in the company of hordes of schoolchildren running riot – and he was a man who was generally happy to see others enjoying themselves.)

That other world exists, even if it seems to belong to the fantastic, I mused as I watched the procession of women moving towards the temple, laden with offerings: those slender, narrow-hipped silhouettes, that measured gait, those colours that resound and conspire together in the light of day – the island unlike anything I had ever seen or imagined.

By the roadside, an old man whose face is carved in ebony, smooth as a mask, and his forehead encircled by a scarlet band. Against a tree, a motionless woman with a child on her hip. At a window, framed against the darkness, the torso of a man draped in saffron.

Whether they are working or resting, seated in front of their wares alongside a ditch, or squatting beneath a hut roof like some spindle-legged wading bird, whether their hands are clasped above their heads in a gesture of offering, or they are standing atop the crown of a palm tree still quivering as it has been cut down, the Balinese have a perfect grace. Walter Spies, a German painter from the 1920s who loved them to the point of abandoning everything to settle among them, attributed this rightness of theirs, the impression of necessity that even the slightest of their movements evokes, to the harmony in which they live with nature. "It is of course the most natural thing in the world, and yet it is the strangest and most unusual, since we have lost the art of living in a landscape without destroying it. We have lost the art of forming an integral part of it, the way flowers and animals do with such grace. Everything in Bali is rich, intricate, complex, elaborate and, at the same time, simple."

Simplicity. The return to a golden age which, here, has never been lost. The shadow of D. H. Lawrence hovers over Bali, even though he never visited the place – he who vigorously defended the notion that body and soul are one and indivisible from the cosmos. "The energy of the individual is filtered through his body, in a perfect distribution," Spies also writes.

The island, a stationary point at the centre of the universe, would seem to have received the gift of eternal youth while the rest of the world grows older. Unless this youthfulness relied upon vigilance and imagination.

Let me explain. The earth and mankind are governed by the same forces – rain, wind, sun, heat and tremors – that agitate the volcanoes and human desires, it's all the same. Aware as we are of their influence at every moment of the day, expressing their rhythms and vibrations in walking and dancing, in music, in work and movement, we clearly recognise that the world and we ourselves are bound together, for better or worse, that the inside and the outside, far from being isolated in disparate systems, participate in the same laws – creation and destruction mixed – and that nature, which surrounds us and lies within us, requires a constant effort if we are to preserve our centre of gravity. The union of the body with nature, the religious sense of belonging to the world.

One can go on theorising, concluding that one has taken a running jump into the legendary, that harmony might be mainly in the eye of the beholder (not that I think so myself), and that reality keeps many a trick up its sleeve, which is what the Balinese believe. What then? Whatever the reasons and the hidden facets, all that beauty is there, undeniable, I can bear witness.

Well, what about the castes, you will say, the Hindu caste system? It still casts a shadow of suspicion over all this fine Balinese harmony. It fixes people in a predetermined social level, the one into which they are born, it imprisons them for life.

That is not entirely true – perhaps not true at all. The English class system which is subtly discriminatory, even if it is supposed to be on the way out, is immeasurably more constrictive than the four wretched Balinese castes: everybody, or very nearly, 90 per cent of the population, belongs to the fourth, the caste of the *sudra* (peasants, artisans). The other three: *brahmana* for scholars and the religious, *satria* for kings and princes, *wesia* for those who serve them, do not imply any lifetime privileges, but merely a recognition of the family line and its permanence.

For it is possible to progress in society, to change trade or marry between castes without losing the mark of one's origin. No more can one lose the memory of one's father, grandfather and all who have preceded him, a continuity from which the Balinese appear to derive – remarkable as this may seem to us with our fixation on equality – not just pride but the reassurance of being inscribed by their lineage into the group, the society, the world, in harmony with the good order of things. No alarming void, no interstellar drift, no frantic effort to define yourself within a society that has little concern with you, then patiently, rung by rung, hoist yourself higher – but your own place reserved from all time and which most people seem to accept, if appearances are to be believed.

At Besakih, where an unofficial guide took us in hand, judging that we needed supervision and explanations, the key to this attitude was supplied to us in the calm self-possession with which our man, affably reticent like many Balinese, answered our indiscreet questions.

"I am a *sudra*," he told us, "and so was my father, and his father before him, and my son will be, as will most of the population."

"And this caste system, does it suit you?"

"Of course. Society works perfectly well this way, I am like

my grandfather and his grandfather before him, and his grandfather before *him*."

So the enumeration continued, we had understood.

"And how is this difference between castes indicated?"

He hesitated for a moment – too many nuances to explain
to curious strangers, especially in pidgin English – then told us
that it was a question of language. Depending on whether a
sudra is addressing a *brahmana* or a fellow *sudra*, he uses a different degree of formality in his language; the former will answer
in appropriate idiom, thus the noble and the common will meet
in their respective replies, contrasting levels and Byzantine
nuances, each endeavouring to come close to the other, or on
the contrary to keep his distance, by means of words which
have their own origin and attribution. It is worth noting that
both parties know how to employ several idioms within the
confines of a single language. So as to discover which idiom to
adopt, nobody will have the egregious vulgarity to ask: "How
do you make your living?" but simply, and more precisely:
"Where do you sit?" a little higher or a little lower?

KLUNGKUNG AND THE PUPUTAN

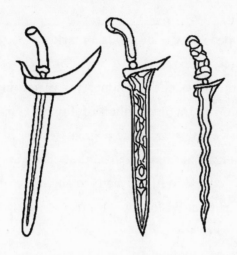

IN THE DAYS BEFORE OUR TRADING POSTS, OUR BUTCHERIES, our ransackings, Klungkung was only a small kingdom, but it was the most important one on the island, numbering several princes. All the other kingdoms were subject to it; they even say that its king, the Dewa Agung or "supreme god" was a direct descendant of the illustrious Majapahit family (though some claim he was born from the amours of a nymph and a stone statue of the god Brahma). The Majapahit reigned over eastern Java from the thirteenth to the sixteenth century, when Islam succeeded in banishing them for good; unlike the Hindus and Buddhists, the Muslims were then relative newcomers and landed first as proselytising and, before long, warring Indian traders. The Hindu court and retainers – the priests, artists and artisans – found refuge with the Dewa Agung and, spurred by the Balinese creative impulse, built the superb palace of Klungkung.

We stopped the car on a little market square opposite the ancient palace, whose delicacy and pomp the guidebooks vie with each other to celebrate, though today nothing of it remains – nothing but the fragile pavilion of Taman Gili, positioned on its pool of sleeping water like a great water lily, forgotten by the modern city that hums all around it. The king and his guard were in the habit of retiring here to meditate and confer, relishing the purifying vision of the green water where hundreds of glossy flowers grew.

The sovereign had only to lift his gaze (just as we did, hapless tourists, applying ourselves to our labours despite the pitiless afternoon sun) and some part of the calm dispensed by the pool would have taken flight: up on the ceiling reigned the maddest agitation, tiny figures jostling and shoving and heaving and fleeing, evidently under the impulse of a frightful panic. They are pursued by a pack of ferocious demons who make Satan and his legions look like amiable jokers. Some of the demons have even caught them: three heads emerge from a seething cauldron beneath which some jesting monsters are stoking up hell's fire; others are busy separating a woman's legs so as to thrust in a flaming brand, a lobster with claws bigger than jaws grabs a breast and twists it, while another torturer, this one human, brandishes a sword over the victim; a couple with a remarkable likeness to Adam and Eve hasten beneath a deluge of arrows . . . the saw, the stake, the lance, the fire and the entire horde of wild beasts to chastise the wicked and the feckless (barren women are forever suckling plump, well-nourished serpents). Incredible comic strips that unsettle the ceiling with that dance of reds, browns and golds, no doubt upsetting the reveries of the king, who surely must have felt himself implicated as well.

Better advised as they were, the Dutch knew to exploit these paintings and introduce some practical activity in a place given over, in their view, to a dubious repose, close to dreaming. They turned the "floating pavilion" into a law court and the Bale Kambang, the adjacent building, into a room where the families of the accused waited. Could it be that they too were brought to judgement for all the crimes they committed in Bali? – every plaintiff on the island would have gathered around the Bale Kambang, the flimsy walls of which, eroded by damp, were not sufficient to hold them all.

In the little museum just a single canvas, but an eloquent one: it shows the Dutch equipped with modern rifles shooting at the Balinese crowd armed only with their krises and spears, "humble weapons that served only to have them die with dignity", as the caption put it. Among the photographs of the Klungkung notables there is one of an arrogant and resolute young girl holding her head high and taking good care not to smile: a princess determined to die "with dignity", and who in fact did die in April 1908, during the mass suicide of Klungkung and its court, known as "the grand finale" or *puputan raya*. With her fell the last independent Balinese kingdom.

The *puputan* of Klungkung, like the earlier one of Badung, inflamed the imagination of European painters and novelists. Of course the Balinese did not accept Dutch control, but what force could have driven them to die together, and moreover to wish for this death and to prepare for it with the most meticulous ritual, leaving its execution to white barbarians who could contrive nothing better than one final act of butchery, and then another?

The day of the massacre, the king, the princes and their retinue had dressed in festive attire and armed themselves with their most beautiful krises; they wore red and black, while the women displayed long white scarves. The children too – excepting those who were too young to walk, and who were carried in their mothers' arms – all held weapons so that they could die with dignity. They came to within a hundred metres of the Dutch rifles, they broke into a run, group after group, more than a thousand of them. "Our troops could hesitate no longer," wrote the chroniclers. So they opened fire.

"While those still alive pressed their assault and our troops kept up a withering fire, the slightly wounded killed off the badly wounded. The women bared their breasts to offer them to the bullets or their backs so that they might be stabbed between the shoulder blades.

"And when we hit the Balinese who were striking at their

fellows, others would arise – men and women – to continue their gory task.

"Many committed suicide . . . Old men would walk among the scattered corpses and slash at the wounded all about until they in turn were killed by the bullets. None of this could be avoided. There was an endless surge of people coming up to continue this labour of destruction."[1]

In a word, the Dutch no longer knew whether they were firing in order to kill or to prevent the killing. Such was their state of disarray.

But even before the Bale Kerta Gosa, there are two guardian statues posted to either side of the entrance, and they signal another danger, this one more recent, and more insidious. In place of the traditional demons the Balinese artist, as though stirred by a premonition, has carved two little bearded men. One of them is wearing a top hat and has a markedly European look about him with his round eyes and protuberant nose. A greedy mouth, neck straining forward, hand counting the coinage, he is the very image of rapacity, a sort of caricature of capitalist usury, prefiguring those property developers and financiers who buy up the precious Balinese land, every inch of which is under cultivation, in order to build sumptuous villas which they rent out or sell for a fortune, one threat among many others that weigh upon the island.

---

[1] H. M. Van Weede, *Indische Reiserinnerungen*, 1908.

61

FROM DENPASAR TO BATUKAU

GIVEN THE BREVITY OF HIS STAY, THE TOURIST IS CONDEMNED to pass through places, not to stop as he would wish, trying each time to capture the spirit of the place, to hold on to its essence in the form of a good thick cluster of memories – not unlike those that the rodent hoards away for the winter. The tourist too will return to these memories in moments of famine or penury: a breakdown in his dreams, his imagination, love or energy, whatever. Does this rapidity imply that his impressions are fragmentary, superficial? Not necessarily. We all recognise that when we travel time dilates until it no longer has any relation to our normal scales; it takes on a different meaning, and our sensitivity takes on a new edge. The same old story: familiarity breeds contempt.

Moreover, should the traveller have the smallest inclination to loosen up, his fresh experiences may well take root in his consciousness and, when he is home again, back among his familiar preoccupations and way of life, they will send him a signal, like a flashing beacon, that he must carry on, keep limbered up, pursue his path and the intuitions he has been able to collect in his moments of receptivity.

How intensely a journey may etch itself in us! We think we are about to make a journey, but before long it is the journey that is making *us* – Nicolas Bouvier, a great travel writer, remarked upon this. Indeed, what is the point of travelling if one doesn't wish to be changed, changed even a little, become detrained from the habit that normally lays too much claim on us? "A step towards less is a step towards better." Bouvier again. For him travel was a form of asceticism, at the end of which he reckoned to acquire – or wanted to acquire – enough transparency to make people see all that he had seen.

This goal joins the earlier one: to show the reader that dazzling stretch of road, to introduce people we have loved and continue to love, to evoke landscapes that swell our hearts with tenderness. To see, which is no small undertaking: it is rather a question of absorption in the observed object to the point of disappearance within it. And to make it seen, if possible.

Day after day we advanced further into the island. Occasionally Sacha would stop to take photographs, which served as a basis for his sketches, and I to record details and impressions, which were so numerous that I was afraid I might see them evaporate.

From Denpasar to Batukau, the volcano in the north of the island, the road climbs vertiginously. As we ascended, the road was being scoured by rain. An hour earlier, the black clouds had burst and a deluge had come down on our heads, drowning the patchwork of paddies all the way to the horizon. We stopped for lunch just as the downpour was beginning to show signs of exhaustion. Nestling on the hillside overlooking the regular planes of water, a bamboo hut perched on stilts and surrounded by its veranda was clearly awaiting our arrival. We reached it by a suspension bridge that made us regret that we had not spent our young years like Tarzan. We found two girls inside, seated at a long wooden table doing their English homework. A row of brand-new bicycles stood waiting for the non-existent tourists (what crazy masochist would want to assault the slopes of Batukau?). Seeing these two wild-eyed scarecrows emerging from the rainstorm, the girls left off their homework and burst into laughter. One of them had black curls and lovely painted lips; both seemed anxious to start a conversation with their few words of English. The usual questions: "Where do you come from?" "Which country?" "Do you know Bali?" France. No, however much they racked their memory, the word meant nothing to them – too small, too far away. Well, how about Paris? Ah, yes, the Eiffel Tower . . . No, they have no wish to go there, to be honest they've never even given it a thought. What about *some* journey? No, that is not one of the things they can imagine, it is an experience beyond the realm of the possible, they are as incapable of grasping the idea of 10,000 francs as we are the idea of a billion dollars, such figures get lost in the clouds. There is no visible wealth in these parts, so it is not mythicised.

For us too Paris seems remote, just a word, light as a wreath of smoke, and as quickly dispersed, so much less real, at present, than the heavy banana leaf with raindrops sliding down it. What do they do all day in this empty restaurant lost amid the rice fields? They wait, they work, this is their life.

Fifteen minutes later they bring us sizzling, smoking kebabs of *sate ayam* on a terracotta piglet laden with burning coals. Outside, the water flows down the mountainside with the rumble of a torrent; a little below our hut, it branches out into a complicated system of channels that cascade from terrace to terrace, irrigating the rice plants down to the bottom of the slope.

Water. A religion of water. All over the island it is to be seen and heard – black water, bottomless, volcanic lakes; stepped mirrors of rice paddies reflecting the sky and dotted with emerald green; limpid water rushing furiously down from the volcanoes; stagnant water of the lotus ponds; jets from fountains in the shadow of the palaces; lustral water from sacred springs welling up from the ground in monstrous bubbles and collected by villagers for their temple rites . . . The sound of running water accompanies every hour of the day. Its music is not all that different from that of the gamelan, about which Debussy (who heard one playing at the Universal Exhibition of 1889) said they were only two things to which he might compare it: "The moon's gleam, and moving water. It is pure and mysterious like the gleam of the moon and ever changing like water in motion." We listened to the gamelan late at night, at Ubud, sitting at the base of a tree in the palace of Sukawati; it seemed to concentrate all the magic of the island in its strange, reedy notes, and we would try in vain to discern its movements – a bass over which the melody fluctuated – to understand why its complex and ever-similar variations produced in us such hypnotic effect; it was as though the voices of the trees and plants were here collected together in the form of a recurrent rhythm instilled with numberless delicate nuances.

Debussy never visited Bali and I have to complete his definition with one by Walter Spies, also a musician, who studied these percussion orchestras and even succeeded in reproducing their scales on the piano: "As one listens to it one has the feeling that something of the luxuriance and depth of the Balinese landscape vibrates in the resonance of the metal and bamboo in a harmony so subtle that it has been transmuted into rhythm."

That day the ceaseless rain reminded me of the notes of the gamelan – isolated drops, regular and insistent, that resound and re-echo.

We were halfway up the mountain, at the site where the Pura Luhur, one of the island's most important temples, had been built. There was a clearing in the heart of the tropical forest, a piece of level ground for the absent cars, but of the temple not a trace. We made for a shack where three Balinese, rejoicing in the rare, comic spectacle of tourists, laughed and laughed as they produced tickets. Beneath their alert gaze I read the prominently displayed notice:

No admittance to the temple for:
Pregnant women [but the Balinese, conscious of good manners, call them "ladies"];
Women whose children do not yet have their first tooth;
Children who have not lost their milk teeth;
Women having their periods [here again, "ladies"];
The impure owing to a death in the family;
Mad women, mad men;
Those improperly dressed.

Finally: Those entering the temple must keep it clean.

It is easy to explain these prohibitions. When tired, preoccupied, labouring under anxieties or crushed by grief (in the case of a bereavement), people are, as it were, divorced from themselves, and their mind is not sufficiently free to allow them to devote themselves to the rites of offering. Furthermore, their inner turmoil has a negative influence on the group. And it is a matter of nothing less than putting up a strong, united front

– an electric charge of maximum power – against the evil spirits who are quick to exploit the slightest weakness or flaw and from there to infiltrate. Every ritual is a means of giving thanks to the gods and recognising their existence, but also of guarding against their fearsome power.

We have been warned. Wrapped in our sarongs, belted with the yellow scarf that confines our agitation beneath the waist, to the lower body, and lucid in spirit, at least in principle, to the extent that the crushing heat and the blinding rain permits, we set off in the direction indicated.

Facing the jungle in the storm light, at the top of a flight of steps, the two outstretched wings of a lava porch – the last remnants of a buried city. And yet no, it is not a question of an opening on to the human world, there is no city hidden in the background of the enchanted domain, plunged in its heavy vegetal sleep: all that shows through the slightly ajar gates of dark stone is the thick greenery of the forest. Then, further off, poised straight over the axis above the line of trees, as though sketched with a heavy charcoal stroke, the sheer, symmetrical slopes of the volcano, Mount Batukau. Threshold, door, passage, entrance, a symbolic sign traced out at the edge of the worlds, gateway as transition, a hyphen that separates and connects them.

We step through and discover the temple, with its numerous *meru*[1] crested with brown palm leaves.

---

[1] An altar with a pagoda roof for the nature divinities.

Before one of them a small group of celebrants has assembled in the rain in festive attire. Priests in golden sarongs are chanting. A woman places her offering at the foot of a sacred banyan and returns to sit with the others. The eldest priest, the one dressed all in white, approaches the faithful who are waiting, motionless, and sprinkles them liberally with sacred water by means of a bouquet of frangipani flowers. They slowly rub their faces with the water, then pass their hands methodically over their heads several times.

All this quietly done, without fuss, among themselves. They seem not to have noticed us.

Not far from there, on an island in the middle of a lake darkened by the density of the trees, a little altar has been erected; adorned with yellow cloth and surrounded with protective parasols, it shelters the presence of an invisible god.

TANAH LOT AND
THE LAKE BRATAN

From the mountain to the sea coast, from the temple of Luhur to the temple of Tanah Lot, the road winds through forests and rice fields. A landscape of green hollows and peaks lost in the clouds. A wild, inextricable space in which these regular stretches of calm water have been unflaggingly carved out, rounded and glinting like silver scales on a fish's back, and edged with narrow margins of grass along which here and there the narrow silhouette of a peasant moved.

Then the villages one passes through, and the temples; and, on the verges of the road, the dominant shades of a green pricked out with flaming reds, crimsons and golds. Points, arrows, spirals, plumes of pink down, spears lined with purple, flowers, clusters, cones, parasols, darts and spurs – the sequence is end-less. The ochre stone of the temples, adorned and eroded by a fluorescent moss, emerges from this jumble of shapes from which it borrows its capricious outlines and inspiration. Highly elab-orate, embroidered, all crests and talons, the whole seems to add up to Nature made concrete, exposing a backdrop that is normally invisible: this hidden aspect that reflects the fears and hopes of men, the dreams and pictures exhumed from the depth of ages or from childhood, suggested by the unconscious mind coming to the surface, monsters and gnomes, fabulous beasts, serpents with tiaras or beneficent dragons, and a whole flight of wings and feathers that point towards the sky and betray a dual allegiance – earth and heaven, profane and sacred – and the high gates stretching into space, extended beyond the limits of possibility, emerging from among the trees like the reminder of the ever-open passage from one world to the next. The marvellous as a constant presence. Ultimately, the essential of existence is not family or career, not the way we perceive our-selves or others perceive us, but this ability to step outside the boundaries of the finite, to surpass the limits of ordinary vision so that an endless vista opens of sightlines and vanishing points, so that the passing moment is charged with life and mystery.

Everywhere on the island where the gods still live this mys-tery is present; gazing at the shapes born of religious imagery, one cannot forget it for a moment. And far from being wit-nesses of some half-buried past – in other words, a dead past –

empty of meaning, like those nostalgic ruins left by vanished civilisations, these forms are assuredly *ever living*, significant and honoured; the offerings prove it. Statues, landscapes and temples attest an imaginative vision, imaginative in William Blake's understanding of the term, the faculty whereby we gain access to a limitless universe.

Tanah Lot is a rocky excrescence. Little brown *merus* with staged roofs, pagoda-style, have been planted on it as a finishing touch, a simple addition that underscores the perfection of the whole. Perched on its rocky islet beaten by the waves, it is round as a mushroom, solitary, self-possessed. A position no doubt required by the merciless struggle against the assaults of the sea, and of the evil gods who lurk therein: out of its base thousands of caves have been dug in strange shapes alongside clumsy pillars. Clumps of vegetation cover it, eddying in a long tress which the serpent-god Basuki, or some sea monster, might seize to haul itself up.

Upon the dark and deep Lake Bratan, atop a crater, the Pura Ulun Danu benefits from the calm of the surroundings and from the protection of a benign goddess – a piece of good fortune not enjoyed by the temple of Tanah Lot in its turbulent waters. One need only compare their architecture to understand the difference in their respective purposes: Tanah Lot is compact, crouched in an attitude of single combat, isolated amid the waves, the very picture of defiance in the face of immensity. Pura Ulun Danu is all lacework and lattice, so that the elements circulate through it – water, air, wind, space inhabit it or rather the temple includes them, welcomes them within its stone projections and the orderly roofs of its *merus*. This one is peaceful and solitary too, and its serenity depends not on digging in but on opening out. A few days earlier we had contemplated it; by the rough sea, its image of repose returned to us.

We sat down at the outermost point of the cliff so that we could see the temple of Tanah Lot in all its splendid isolation. On this narrow ledge we thought we would be at peace. Little did we know! Somehow a tourist slipped in and planted herself right in front of us to take photographs. She was an unprepossessing redhead (not her fault); her broad bottom obtruded very precisely between us and the sublime panorama, in fact it completely blocked out our view (absolutely her fault). We were seized by the temptation, fleeting but powerful, to revert to extinct rites and offer a sacrifice to the gods of the sea. One little shove, only one. Eventually Sacha made do with a few well-chosen words, the tone of which seemed to hit harder than their import. With the aplomb of people conscious of their rights, she answered in her best English (or American or Australian): "Anyone is entitled to take pictures. After all, this is a tourist zone." A tourist zone, much as one might speak of a playground, or a shopping mall . . . administrative divisions, motorways and car parks, giant supermarkets and mass consumption regulated by planners, organised by an all-powerful publicity machine. The down-to-earth West with its conditioned reflexes vs.

millennial Asia. The sense of the sacred is eliminated, demons and gods with their infinite, subtle presence are expunged. Here we are, back to a functional distribution of space, everything in its place, parked safely in its designated slot, with a view to maximising productivity, with dreams and sensations as part of the package – provided that they behave themselves.

It is not a question of looking, still less of being steeped in a state of mind, but of applying oneself conscientiously to one's job as a tourist, in the area set aside for this activity. Action, output, film. Film is spooled off by the yard like a barrier broadening between the living object and our imagination. Confronted with all this bustle, contemplation is out of place . . . Our tourist is practically bursting with indignation; she turns her back on us and nobly stalks off to take her pictures elsewhere. Let us, between ourselves, set the record straight: we should take a little comfort, remind ourselves that we have right on our side – even if such an assurance does not go far against the weight of numbers.[1]

Why shouldn't particular sites, which over the generations have been the repositories of hopes, fears, prayers and supplications, enjoy the same right to a little consideration as the people who continue to honour them – not a full agreement, that would be asking too much, but at least some measure of

---

[1] Proof enough that the tourists have got it right: a gigantic luxury hotel has been built here for the benefit of the better off among them, despite the resistance of the Balinese, for whom this site is sacred.

attention? Landscapes are not merely snapshots to take home: they have something to say to us. One has only to be quiet and lend an ear, and one may hear their mute language.

But the tourist has no time to listen, barely even time to look: he is taking photographs. He does not set his brain to work: he points his camera, he has been led to believe that this is the surer option. Mechanics have replaced the organ of sight, a photograph in place of a recollection, the solidity of paper rather than the fleeting mental picture.

It is true that impressions get forgotten while a photograph can be kept. In this frantic, pathetic desire to fix the moment, to miss nothing, to lose nothing, there is a sort of fear, indeed of enslavement: it is the need, soon an obsessive one, to profit to the utmost (make no mistake, this is much more a duty than a pleasure), to take full advantage of what one has earned and truly deserved – a voyage – to seize this exceptional and transient fragment of life and fix it against oblivion, to possess it for all time, who knows whether another chance will ever come along? The only possible response to such a tremendous imperative is to entrust it to the camera, which is more reliable than our capricious memory, or so the advertisements tell us. A Herculean labour. Nobody is up to it, everyone achieves it in his fashion. The sharing out too: to each his own – some rely on their cameras and display their snapshots, others rely on their senses, and they jot a few lines.

So much for our red-haired tourist with her aura of sadness.

We forget her, her shamelessness and her photos of Tanah Lot. She was no more absurd than that group of Japanese I saw one day in a church in Italy. The nave was in complete darkness and they went galloping past the side chapels, peppering the invisible paintings with their cameras as they went; the church was illuminated by their flashbulbs. They left the building relieved: the paintings, if any existed, they would inspect back home, sitting among friends in the comfort of their armchairs.

THE MONKEY FOREST

WE LEFT AT FIRST LIGHT AND THE DAY STRETCHED OUT BEFORE us. It had no end. Occasionally the sun peeped through the clouds; by the time we had returned to the car we were quite stunned, dazzled by it. Having left the car in the shade of the trees the previous day, we now tottered into it for refuge, to get our breath back and study the map and our route: Tabanan, Kerambitan, Wangayegede, the names alone set us dreaming. At the first turning, the shops lining the road that opened before us, the puttering of the motor scooters setting off to tackle the city . . . the morning was beginning, it was brand new – and so were we.

Between Ubud and Kerambitan, in the monkey forest, where the foliage is thickest, lurks a temple. Lit by a submarine light, devoured by moss and lichen, the temple has a ruined look, a look of catastrophe, of an eerie apparition. We did not, however, have the leisure to indulge in lengthy reflections. The sacred monkeys are at liberty to move about the jungle; they are big greyish macaques who long ago lost the habit of group living, in an unexceptionable savage state. The dapper white tourist walking in all innocence towards the temple seems to offer far more interesting company than their own kind. Posted at the corner of a pathway or on a branch within head's reach, these highwaymen keep an eye on him, feigning total unconcern. They know what they're up to: they need only show a touch of aggression – these monkeys have nerve – to frighten the visitor, a ready-made fall guy, and get their share. Just what that is remains to be seen – trinket or ear lobe. The visitor, who is doubtless at ease in an office or on a beach, cuts a sorry figure when it comes to man-to-man combat. He already looks rather idiotic and gauche out in the wild. Still, he has stocked up with peanuts on the way in, as he has been advised to do, and with this safe conduct he imagines he is secure, more or less. Little does he know, but he will scarcely have time to proceed to the ritual offering.

A guide had obligingly told me that the sacred animals like spectacles and earrings, so it would be as well to surrender them without delay and let the monkeys have their eats, the vendors are there after all to help you. I had, however, observed an unfortunate Malay tourist who had followed these instructions to the letter, but had still been forced to flee. He had bought his bag of food at the ticket office and turned towards the woods when a score of large and small monkeys, their teeth bared, accosted him in combat formation. In sheer panic, his salutary reflex made him fling the bananas and peanuts as far as he could, then sprint away.

The Malay tourist had scarpered like a hare. Cautioned by his example, I had bought nothing and, with no ornament or protection for my face, I walked in relative tranquillity. Suddenly I felt a tug at my skirt. It was not a request but an order. In spite of a certain amount of preparation, man has no idea what the law of the jungle really is. It is not a question of bluffing or arguing, of explaining or buying time: when confronted with a stronger body, we do as bidden. It's simple enough. The monkey – for that is what it was, a sizeable macaque, with a commanding eye and imposing stomach, seeing that I kept it waiting – not for nothing – leapt straight on to my shoulders. Benefiting from his superior position, he was feeling my face carefully with his hard, coarse paws, sniffing, inspecting, examining the possibilities. Sacha, unaccustomed to such a spectacle, took out his camera and asked me to smile. Final humiliation, the monkey, finding nothing at all enticing on offer, with a second negligent leap returned to the ground and left to pursue more promising quarry.

A moment later we heard the prolonged shriek of an Australian lady some three metres behind us.

THE PURI AGUNG WISATA

LEAVING THE MONKEY FOREST WITHOUT REGRET, WE DROVE on towards Kerambitan, where the royal family of Tabanan has one of its palaces.

More often than not, when we stopped in a village, people took no notice of us; they carried on with their duties, like the barefoot, stooped old woman who was sweeping up the dead leaves in the first courtyard of the palace. As we passed in front of her, she raised her head, gave us a smile, and with an ample and gracious gesture invited us to step within, then continued sweeping. Occasionally people would look at us and laugh, whether from sheer pleasure, as we were politely assured, or from their sense of the comic: those white faces, those "pointed noses" (a peculiarity of Westerners), that touching and awkward eagerness to please by adopting the island's habits and customs. A sort of silent commentary, at all events, an awareness of the total difference. Personally, I lean towards the comic interpretation: no need to look further than at a mural in the Pura Maduwe Karang, in the north of the island, and the way that local sculptors have immortalised Nieuwenkamp, a Dutch artist who tended to travel about on his bicycle. We see only a mole's proboscis probing from a multitude of round flowers; the bicycle's wheels, gears and all, are likewise transmuted into a mass of petals. Or there are Dutchmen, this time in a painting, sociably knocking back their tankards of beer – corpulent, heavy and jovial, as Brueghel rendered them. Or else those clownish figures of *wayang golek*, obese Europeans, with long noses and big hats . . . All this with plenty of humour and not a grain of malice.

The Indonesian view of the white man clearly still includes some element of the vulgarity ascribed to those *punokawan*, of the loutishness of those "kings from beyond the seas" who, in the *wayang* equally, constitute the very antithesis of oriental refinement. A shortage of courtesy, of tact: the white man is a complete peasant, a *kasar*, that is, he lacks subtlety, he remains a barbarian through and through. He is direct, abrupt, no beating about the bush, he wants fast results; all this perplexes a people for whom everything is a question of echoes, of oblique, measured approaches.

"Here," Sacha observed, "there is no need to speak in order to be understood."

Our home was a few hundred metres outside Kerta, and the villagers came willingly to lend us a hand when we faced practical problems – problems so frequent, it must be confessed, that they threatened to floor us: disrupted water supply, electricity failure, lack of provisions or ignorance of local products, all manner of things. When they first saw us arrive, the villagers had smiled at us – that broad, trusting smile that the Balinese address to strangers before they start wondering about them. Then, coming to look at us, they were curious, friendly, unintrusive. We spoke to them in a few words of English. But words were unnecessary for them to understand us – we would in any event have been hard put to make our meaning clear this way – gestures were sufficient. The direction of a glance, an inchoate movement was enough, or those constant unwitting signs that betray a taste, or a habit. Our neighbours knew how to grasp and interpret them – unless, of course, they possessed the science of divination, as I was sometimes tempted to believe; at any rate they had this intuition that allows a person to perceive a wish or a buried emotion as clearly as others make out the colour of the sky or sniff the direction of the wind. Otherwise, how do we explain that they arrived at the precise moment that we needed them, or suggested a stroll when we were bored, or brought a gardenia, branch and all, that Sacha had been wanting to draw, and answered questions we had not even formulated yet? We soon fell into the habit of watching our intonation when we were talking between ourselves, and also the expression we wore, lest they pick up an unintended message. Thus in the absence of language did we sustain a dialogue all in nuances, compounded of tiny but revealing things. We were delighted with our progress, for it showed us that we and our neighbours were arriving at a form of entente. A small step forward in our understanding of the island.

To return to the Westerner, who remains a stranger – we had no illusions on this subject – another point against him is his reluctance to acknowledge the merits of any system not his own, "his attachment to inherited values which he believes to be universal and infallible".[1] A superiority complex whose underlying reasons sometimes prove impenetrable.

Faced with such oddity, humour is an instinctive reaction, humour rather than simple mockery that implies judgement and denial. Humour is the reflex that novelty provokes in the Balinese: here is a laughter that it is possible to share. The islanders do not wish to offend the visitor: they simply chuckle. In their shoes we would do exactly the same, but not so gently. Perhaps the Balinese feel so remote from the tourist and his curious lifestyle that they cannot imagine it, and thus feel no envy of his existence: they have no need to appropriate it for themselves. What we possess, technical know-how, hardly seems

---

[1] Denys Lombard, *Le Carrefour javanais*, Vol. I, EHESS, 1990.

to fascinate them. What they possess does captivate us, we who are at a dead end: sensitivity saturated by Information, this kind of absent-minded and approximate culture, an impoverished imagination atrophied by a ceaseless force-feeding of the concrete. A sort of spiritual aridity, in effect.

No recipe for survival, however, just recourse to the memory guarding the deposit of images that look more like the fragments of a dream – maybe the embodiment of an inner vision – than like a recognised reality.

They have about them an intensity that haunts you: those extravagant shapes, those exaggerated colours, the superabundant vegetation – so many spaces of enchantment open to the very horizon of the real, where the frontiers get blurred. On the island, the impressions made by nature have the power to shake the spirit, to penetrate it deeply. The imaginary shows itself at every turn, as in a half-waking dream, at the edge of hallucination. Take the rooms of the palaces: they open on to the stifling heat of the jungle and are as materially evident to the five senses as they are to the wildest imagination. The boundaries separating the two worlds are erased; we pass from one to the other without quite knowing where we are, or to which we belong. To feel that the limits that usually hem us in have vanished into thin air, evaporated like steam under the combined effects of art and nature, is to feel a wonderful sense of liberation.

This sensation of marvel, perhaps I felt it most strongly in this palace of Kerambitan, the Puri Agung Wisata. The palace was empty. With a wave of her wand the old fairy – she of the dead leaves – had shown us into a deserted place, one fast asleep.

We proceeded from room to room, or rather from court-yard to courtyard, without seeing a soul. These enclosures were bordered by vast rooms set on tall plinths. Only the terraced part was visible, the part facing outward and open to view, the rest being shut away in its intimacy by an exquisitely worked little door.

In the first courtyard a fountain warbled; in their hanging cages birds – cockatoos, mynahs and turtle doves – watched us without a peep, their gossip no doubt interrupted at the fairy's first bidding. We passed in silence in front of a state room with sumptuously gilded furniture. Everything was ready and waiting for a guest of honour who was late arriving: the low table laden with flowers and a tea tray, the sugar bowl well filled and fine porcelain cups. On the wall, neatly ordered in their frames, the portraits of the masters of the place: the rajah and his family, upright and dignified, a splendid group looking towards an invis-ible horizon.

Encircling these rooms that stood forever rooted in a posi-tion of attention, the jungle exploded in red and green bou-quets, in flowers, clusters, strange pendants. Maybe they were there as a defence against its threats, those two giant toads bearing parasols which stood guard to either side of the narrow door, at the far end of the salon, concealing further mysteries?

The opening to the second courtyard was half hidden behind a thick curtain of blue orchids. Intimidated by so much apparently purposeless splendour, we tiptoed in, like the bewildered visitor in *Beauty and the Beast*. This compound was occupied by the rajah's wives: on their pedestal, we saw nothing but beds covered with fine fabrics, while magnificently patterned plates encrusted every wall.

At this moment, I believe – for we had lost all sense of reality – a young man came towards us and smilingly asked if he could help us. He was one of the princes of the palace – handsome, as was to be expected, with the brownest eyes and the whitest teeth. The fairy tale remained true to form, the episodes following in a decidedly orderly succession.

We were indeed in the courtyard of the wives of the king, his father. The end room, the most spacious one, was reserved for women born into the family: on this bed, generation after generation, they had come to die – it was the room for the final act of life. His father had had five wives and four sons: he himself was the youngest. Meeting him today in this palace, which he oversaw to help the rajah, was mere chance, he told us, for he was often away on his travels.

On reaching this point in his story the prince decided to modify it a little, introducing a touch of modernity by evoking the New World. He was often in New York, he had even travelled there as a steward on a liner, after being hired by a friend of his. However, he invariably returned to Bali. His brothers were married here, lived here, and in a moment he would show us their wives' residence.

The transition between the two worlds was brought about smoothly; it had taken but the name of a city and a prince who had become a ship's steward to conquer America, the ever-youthful, the ever-beautiful.

We were following him across a succession of courtyards. "Here is the palace temple, you see there's a Mercedes in it" – there was indeed a large, grey motor car of an antique model, parked next to the two traditional statues in their black-and-white check sarongs – "but for a Balinese, putting a motor car inside a temple is not a problem: they have created a god of cars, also a god of money. The black-and-white-chequered sarong indicates that good and evil live side by side, that every-thing may be harmoniously blended, we have gods for the most common eventualities of daily living . . ." He smiled gently without for a moment scoffing at our foreigners' naïvety, for all that we were in fact somewhat taken aback by this intrusion of the sacred into areas generally considered to be profane. Some of the larger courtyards were hired out for receptions and con-ferences, but the villagers also came whenever there was a feast at the palace.

Thus the modern world of business infiltrated this kingdom beyond time. The Balinese are surprisingly adaptable, taking from the outside world whatever is of value while preserving their own culture and traditions. This amiable and exquisitely courteous young man, a guide at one moment and a prince the next, was the living proof of this. We suggested making some offering towards the upkeep of the palace, however modest; he accepted with a smile, with a smile he thanked us for the sum – quite derisory if one considers what he had offered us – which we gave him as we left. To this day I still wonder whether we'd done the right thing.

UBUD AND ITS VISIONARY HERO, WALTER SPIES

BETWEEN THE MONKEY FOREST AND THE TROGLODYTE CAVE of Goa Gajah lies Ubud; its art galleries and shops crammed with knick-knacks are spread out along the main street.

If it is right to tie the memory of a town to the one person who has loved it the most, one may affirm, without much risk of error, that Ubud still belongs to Walter Spies, whose story is told, embellished and re-embroidered by those vigilant Balinese. But it could be that Spies' passion for Bali turns up and discloses the island's legendary quality. His passion has the necessary scope, it reflects, it contains all that is remarkable and tragic about the island.

Allusions to the name of Spies and his Indonesian adventure are often labelled with the idiotic word "idyll" (even "Balinese idyll", to make it complete), just as the label "paradise" attaches to the island of Bali. Amused disdain, condescension. And the ever-present fear of being duped, whether by appearances or by wishful thinking – which makes one the biggest dupe of all. To what purpose this mockery? Because Spies was a happy man and dared to say so in speech and in writing? It must immediately be understood that this state arose from simple-mindedness, or from blindness, for if you fall in love with a country and find yourself at peace in it and preach this from the housetops (that is, if you see everything through rose-tinted glasses), you have to be an imbecile or at any rate a harmless dreamer, which comes to the same thing. Me, I think that Spies, getting away from Germany in the 1920s and from his prison in the Urals, must have been dazzled by what he discovered here: refinement, beauty, a tolerance that could accommodate folly as easily as constraints. Furthermore, he had a feeling for happiness, which was rare enough. Society, far from tolerating him, took care to make him pay.

At Tjampuhan, above Ubud, the Rajah of Sukawati had given him a piece of land on which he built a house. The caretaker, an affable little man with lopsided features like a grotesque mask, escorted us to it without for a moment ceasing to chatter happily and smile. Living as he did in the shadow of Spies, he knew the man well, spoke of him every day; visitors pay as much as $125 a night simply to occupy his room and stir the recollections; for the others, those seeking only nature and reclusion, it costs but $70.

Spies' house is a simple hut with a thatched roof, clinging to the slope of the ravine and hemmed in by trees of dizzy height. There is a single room with a terrace in front of it, where he slept on a mattress on the ground, and behind which a studio served for his painting.

No water supply, no electricity at the time but, down below, the noise of the river, which swells up in the rainy season and, all about, the virgin forest with the lightning flashes of red and yellow flowers, and walls of wild orchids armed with spikes, like scorpions. To judge by the babble of our genial guide, Spies lived among his *objets d'art* and his birdcages, but he also kept some tame monkeys and vampire bats, which slept during the day, heads down, wrapped in their great brown membranous wings. And he shut himself away for days and weeks to paint, only leaving his den when he was completely played out. Even following this regime, each painting required so many hours' work that he could not satisfy demand but was constantly two or three keenly awaited canvases behind schedule. He was recognised all over Europe, everyone desired to own a work of his, the little man proudly assured us. Communing in the memory of Spies who, he told us, loved the Balinese as we did, we became friends with the caretaker. "Tuan Tepis," he said respectfully, the protector of painters, the best loved of Europeans, much more than anyone else, "he has enriched the colour of our dreams."

Today on the land the rajah gave him other houses have intruded, not all that many, each looking like Spies' hut. Like migrating birds who have abandoned their flock, a handful of drop-outs and eccentrics dreaming of paradise have sought refuge here. From their room they see only the trees climbing up the steep slopes in serried ranks, right up to the palm trees on the crest, whose dark tracery is silhouetted against the white sky. And right in the middle of this unkempt vegetation, in those huts open to all the rains, they seem to be attached to some invisible hook and dreaming perhaps that, like Tarzan, they need only seize a creeper in front of their window to revert to a state of primeval innocence.

Way below, in the deepest hollow of the gorge, the unexpected luxury of a swimming pool, a turquoise punctuation mark amid the raw crimson of the hibiscus. Further off, along the riverside, accessible by a slippery stone staircase, there is a cave with monkeys and monsters carved in it.

Apart from the walls of his prison, this was the last stage set that Spies beheld. He had been born in Moscow in 1895, into a family of German diplomats. Thence he went to Dresden for his studies, but had the unfortunate idea of returning to Moscow on holiday with his parents just as the First World War broke out. So he celebrated his twentieth birthday in a prison camp in the Urals. Spies was a late-developing romantic, forever

dreaming of paradise, and he lacked History's sense of time –
a failing for which History never ceased to reproach him. Being
imprisoned in the Urals was only the first rebuke.

But far from heeding the warning, he took full advantage
of the situation to study the lie of the land as a painter, to listen
to the songs of the Tartars and Kirghiz as a musician; he learned
to dance after the Russian fashion and succeeded in entertaining
both friends and foes.

That was not all. As a fifteen-year-old in Dresden he had
been shown how to paint like the cubists and expressionists,
then in the ascendant. But after looking at the landscape of the
Urals, he had the idea of going about it differently, of abandoning this avant-garde that didn't suit him; instead he would
practise an art that tended towards the simplicity of Chagall or
Klee, in whom he recognised kindred spirits. At the end of his
internment, he had developed his own style (influenced also by
the discovery of Douanier Rousseau, "the Sunday painter", a
little later, still in Russia).

His paintings, some of them jealously preserved in the gallery
at Agung Rai, convey the vision of a man whose heart had
found a place to its liking. Nature is minutely represented – the
silken rice paddies festooned with brown velvet, the extravagant palms underlined with light, the yokes of oxen pulling the
ploughshare, with the solitary figure of their driver. But, on
closer inspection, the planes are superimposed in defiance of all
realism: perched in the trees at the heart of a bright aura, a

village crops up like an apparition; branches are pulled aside to reveal a lost countryside. Chimera? Illusion? No road leads to it, unless it be the eternal road of the marvellous. The light and shade tell their own story, that of the legendary island, just as it *exists* in its essential character (for Spies, working from the starting point of his affinities, has learnt how to *see*, how to bring out the magic intrinsic to the landscape). It is rather easy, and wrong, to reduce his vision to an Asian version of German romanticism. The island of Bali has given substance to our ghosts and our dreams. It is not even that we sense or divine the invisible: it is there, scarcely hidden in nature, represented, embodied, we need only open our eyes.

Out there his painting was appreciated for its "mystical impressionism". Asia, as the Surabaya journal continued, was seen in its "spiritual aspect", which was otherwise seldom considered.

After the First World War, Spies returned to Dresden. He took art lessons from Oskar Kokoschka, met Otto Dix; he mixed also with musicians, including Busoni, Haba, Hindemith, Krenek, Pfitzner; and he studied piano with Arthur Schnabel, which was no small honour.

Then he became assistant to F. W. Murnau. Leaving Hellerau, he joined the film director in his villa at Grunewald, where a piano was put at his disposal so that he could exploit the discoveries that he had made in the Urals. Together they travelled, schemed – to make a film on the South Seas – discussed possible uses of light and shade to heighten dramatic tension. They were close to each other and distance never separated them. When the moment came – Spies was then in the antipodes – Murnau gave his protégé financial support while Spies painted his *Traumlandschaft* for him. Later, Murnau was to leave him a good share of his possessions.

The photographs that Spies would take in Bali (they, more than anything else, made him famous) clearly bear Murnau's stamp. Nosferatu, the shadow of evil, spreads himself across the world, the very incarnation of terror. Eyes bulging, fangs sharpened, clawlike nails of monstrous length, the demons of Bali, as Spies saw them, had a family resemblance to vampires. Witches haunt the night, ready to kill; they brandish their raptors' talons, and only magic can conquer them; priests sprinkle the cataleptic dancers with lustral water. Spies, however, by no means invented these demons. From one end of the planet to the other, human terror has found expression in similar imagery, somewhat simplified instruments: deformed by savage emotion, exaggeratedly enlarged, eyes, nails, teeth, a build far and away too tall and indistinct. Spies was content just acknowledging these similarities: his masks looming out from the thickness of the mist, sombre, flickering silhouettes, bearers of darkness and death. To heighten the sense of terror, he would photograph them from below, lying on the ground amid the smoke.

But then his adventure was only beginning. As with Gregor Kraus, another photographer who had preceded him to Bali,

Spies found post-war Europe, for all his prospects, a dreary, cramped place, narrow-minded and puritan, with its laws repressing homosexuality. He felt ill at ease there, he needed space, freedom. In 1923, he decided to leave.

We come upon him next in Java, scraping a living in Bandung by tinkling on a piano in a Chinese cinema. He is instantly swept off his feet by Asia. The Javanese are "incredibly beautiful, aristocratic, refined to their fingertips" (indeed they are, and, coming from Europe, it is easy to understand Spies' amazement), while the Dutch, the occupants for more than three centuries, are "common, uncouth, brutish, narrow-minded, pretentious". He resents the colonists' shoddy treatment of the natives, for the latter, one cannot fail to notice, are by far the superior race. Spies predicts a conflict before long, and here again, he is not wrong. Straightaway he learns Javanese and studies the gamelan, another discovery for him. He cycles about, he paints. Happiness. Or something close to it.

A few weeks later he's at Yogyakarta, and this is when legend takes over. The rajah is going to give a great feast at the *kraton* in honour of a visit by the President of the Philippines. Spies' small orchestra is invited. This is the first time Spies has entered the palace – and he imagines he has stepped into a fairy tale. There is a whole succession of magnificent doorways in painted, carved wood, giant serpents and dragons, passages and corridors, loggias and verandas; he crosses sumptuous gardens dominated by the lordly banyan tree with its "roots climbing into the sky", and passes the old palace servants in their brocaded livery, and the princes, all young and resplendent . . . up to the moment when, already dazed by so much beauty, he reaches the great central hall.

Seated on his throne, the king fans himself. Along the walls his wives wait, barefoot, in silence, simple and beautiful. Then the Europeans arrive: overweight and clumsy in their Parisian outfits, they serve to offset the refinement of these "demigods". The gamelan strikes up. And then the dancing girls advance from the bottom of the garden with measured gait towards the throne: four girls, the most exquisite ever seen, four Egyptian queens, their perfect faces as smooth as masks, devoid of expression, as though stylised. Spies is in ecstasy. But his turn is coming: "You can imagine," he wrote to his mother, "how much I wanted to hammer out fox-trots on the piano to see these great mounds of Dutch flesh quiver." The contrast must indeed have been striking.

But now the sultan, intrigued by an interest which, until then, he had never encountered among Europeans, makes enquiries about this young fair-haired German who seems so fascinated by the gamelan and the dances.

The following day – Spies could not believe his eyes – the carriages of the princes and their retinues drew up in front of his modest hotel with all the pomp intended for the major feasts, and dozens of servants advanced towards him bearing salvers and golden parasols. The sultan asked if Spies would consent to conduct his court dance band: some forty musicians who, according to Spies, nearly all possessed perfect pitch and extremely acute senses. To have his apartment at court among these demigods, to become Javanese, to learn the elaborate codes of oriental courtesy . . . Spies could not believe his luck. A supplementary sign of Fate – but his cup was already so full, it was almost laughable: that same evening at the palace, an old, enormously wealthy Chinaman asked him to paint his mother's portrait.

Spies was the only European authorised to live within the walls of the *kraton*. For four years he lived with one of the princes of the palace, probably his lover, Raden Tummenggung Djojodipuro, who taught him the secrets of court life and the manifold subtleties of Javanese culture. For four years he fulfilled his duties, even finding the means to recreate on his piano the scales so particular to gamelan music. The court made much of him.

But one fine day the Punggawa of Ubud, Prince Tjokorda Gedé Raka Sukawati, invited Spies to visit his island, Bali. And once again Spies was conquered: Bali seduced him more even than Java had done. This time it was the *coup de foudre,* no question about it – Spies was skewered there like the butterfly in its case. "I cannot bear to be away from Bali for more than a month; I am so homesick for it I simply have to go back."

In 1927, Spies therefore took his leave of the Sultan of Yogyakarta and moved to Bali. "He took with him a piano, a German bicycle and a butterfly net," Prince Sukawati explained.

"We would go from one valley to the next, catching butterflies; we would put them in large gilt boxes and send them away to the museums of Europe and all over the world." Thus began Spies' life on Bali, hunting butterflies with Prince Sukawati, who soon gave him a plot of land and a house.

Festivals, dances, temples, religious rites, statues, villages and forests, there was not a place on the island that Spies did not visit, not a ritual he neglected to watch, not a sculpture whose origin was unknown to him, not a village whose inhabitants he failed to befriend. For all that he admired the culture of this country, it was he who would soon revolutionise Balinese painting, hitherto devoted exclusively to the depiction of gods and heroes. His innovation was the result of a chance meeting with a young man, Anak Agung Gedé Soberat, who had been watching Spies on the sly. "Why not, for a slight change, paint what you see around you? A woman selling her merchandise in the market, for instance, or a peasant leading his buffalo amid the rice fields?" This advice was to bear fruit, but that is another story.

Invitations pour in from every side. Emissaries arrive in high excitement to tell him of a festival about to take place. Spies jumps into his ancient car, drives to some remote village, people rush to welcome him, they surround their *Tuan* Spies of Ubud and he greets his *sobat*, friends.

So much so that little by little he becomes the acknowledged authority on Bali, the obligatory point of reference, an object of curiosity. His fame spreads. Bali is now fashionable. Painters, musicians, novelists in search of inspiration come to learn from him, and make free use of his work, a passion that everyone draws on at will. Rich and/or intellectual Europe alights on Bali. Barbara Hutton offers Spies a swimming pool. Charlie Chaplin claims to be fascinated by "his love for Bali and his devotion to the natives". The Duke and Duchess of Sutherland invite themselves to Spies' hut (and afterwards tour the islands aboard their proud yacht). The Dutch settlers realise that the man could be of use to them (he will be naïve enough to believe that his services will earn him gratitude). A museum is established at Denpasar, and he is appointed curator. During the viceroy's visit, Spies is put in charge of the festivities. Later, he is put in charge of promoting the image of Bali overseas, and is asked to contribute to the Colonial Exhibition of 1931 (when Artaud is to discover Bali just as Walter Spies had seen and defined it). True, Spies was reproached with having come to the island burdened with a European heritage that inevitably informed his outlook, and of having therefore altered the "true" Balinese reality, there on the spot, among the Balinese (as if his detractors had the slightest notion of what constituted this reality), but also of falsifying its image abroad; his book *Dance and Drama in Bali*, in which he detailed his particular vision, modified European conceptions of the theatre. A flow of influences embracing the continents.

Spies had no such ambition. For a start, evenings in dress clothes bored him. He would fade to the point of being but a shadow of himself. On returning to his monkeys after one of these extravaganzas, he was reputed to have muttered: "At last, something human." It was said that he did not seem conscious of his personality, that he lacked the narcissism that commands others' attention, that he never sought to assert himself. Photographs reveal a finely chiselled face beneath a helmet of blond hair; his expression is taciturn, reserved, slightly defiant. "As he arrived on the island, Spies may already have been largely concerned with *being*, not with doing or becoming, which are the principal driving forces in the West. Simply to be, like the lake that reflects the sky, or the tree shaken by the wind . . . but also to feel himself being, which the pressure of industrial society in Europe never permits. He flees so that he can create in all tranquillity and devote himself to the luxury of a life in which he has nothing to prove to anybody, except perhaps to himself. Most of all, he flees to a world that satisfied his aesthetic sense."[1]

But Walter Spies was not one of those people permitted to live in peace, not even on an island at the end of the world. With the flood of visitors, Tjampuhan had become unlivable: he could no longer paint. In 1937, he bought a hut perched at the end of a slippery road, on the slopes of the Gunung Agung, at Iseh, halfway between Ubud and Karangasem. There at last

---

[1] Claire Holt, quoted in Hans Rhodius, *Schönheit und Reichtum des Lebens, Walter Spies*, L. J. C. Boucher/The Hague, 1964

he was alone with his painting. Furthermore, he looked out over a sublime vista of rice fields. Forgetting the world, he was able to believe that the world had forgotten him. Retreat, Arcadia. He had escaped from time, from the "nightmare of history". Hitler's Germany and the threat of war, the hostility of the Dutch officials (who envied Spies his rapport with the Balinese), all this was kept far away, at arm's length, a closed bracket.

While Spies was away up his mountain, painting, Holland was alarmed by Germany's activities. The Dutch authorities in Bali suddenly felt vulnerable and naturally sought a scapegoat. What they had tolerated for years now seemed to threaten an order that was all the more precious since it had become imperilled. So the Dutch instigated a witch hunt against homosexuals, orchestrated by a defamatory press campaign. Arrest warrants, searches, denunciations, police raids – no stone unturned. More than a hundred suspects in the colony were arrested, and many more harassed. Suicides, broken marriages, wrecked careers, escapes and total prostration – a chain reaction. The Balinese, who considered homosexuality nothing more than an agreeable pastime, were most perplexed by all this agitation. As for Walter Spies, he refused to believe in the march of history or in human wickedness.

But in the dawn of the new year, 1938, they came to arrest him. His Balinese friends gathered under his prison window at Denpasar to play the gamelan. "Certain officials have concluded that they have an interest in appearing offended by an unconventional German" – such was their sober assessment. They still liked to believe that Spies would be released. But the ever-zealous viceroy had decided to stick to the letter of the law: being miles from civilisation was all the more reason to maintain order. This pressure, added to the long-standing jealousy of certain officials, culminated in Spies being put on trial: he was accused of sexual relations with a minor. His friends, including the anthropologist Margaret Mead and the painter Rudolf Bonnet, pleaded his cause with eloquence, decrying the puritanism of the West, not least in the matter of homosexuality. But all to no end. Spies was found guilty and transferred to Java, into the prison at Surabaya, where he was held until 1939. He used the occasion to translate some Balinese tales and he painted tirelessly: some of his best canvases date from this period. Eventually, he was released. Rejoicing of friends, gamelan and festivities, a whole Spies jubilee. Once again he declared that life was marvellous, "a great big birthday party". And, he threw himself there and then into a fresh exploration with the help of Professor Baas Becking, Curator of the Botanical Gardens at Bogor. This time his subjects were insects and marine life. Spiders, dragonflies, strange spindly starfish, wasps and bees: gouaches and sketches, precise to the point of surrealism, in the style of Dürer on a neutral background, without any of the grass or violets, they poured out thick and fast. Spies piled it in.

The fact was that his time was running out, even if he did not yet realise it. The Second World War broke out, Germany invaded the Netherlands. The Germans left in Indonesia were arrested. Spies had withdrawn to an island in vain: however remote, it still featured on the map of the world at war. But Spies did not live with the map of the world before his eyes, he was forever painting butterflies in his hut at Iseh, obstinately refusing to take any notice of history. He was frogmarched into it one evil day in June 1940: they removed him from his island and placed him in a prisoner-of-war camp on Sumatra.

When Sumatra was threatened by Japan, in 1942, the Dutch crammed their prisoners on board the *Van Imhoff*, a vessel bound for Ceylon. The next day the ship was hit by a Japanese bomb and started to go under. The Dutch crew abandoned ship, and the captain did not presume to order the freeing of the Germans. That was the end for Spies, drowned in the bottom of a hold of a boat slowly sinking into the ocean.

History and society, both of which he had tried to escape, caught up with him twice. His romantic fate and the island of Bali, where he pursued his dream of happiness, both rest on the back of the turtle floating in the middle of the seas. If you wish to approach the legendary beast, you would do well to follow, like a secret path, his turbulent life story.

The life of Spies, the stern silhouette of Rudolf Bonnet, or the pictures hung on the walls of the Puri Lukisan: so many pictures, so many ways to land on Balinese soil without going too far astray.

PURI LUKISAN,
THE PICTURE GALLERY

THE SMALL RECTANGLE OF JUST ONE OF THESE PAINTINGS IS like the concentrated essence of the country's imagination. Rats and mice, tortoises, lizards, snakes, slugs and other small creatures, slithering and busy, snails and dragonflies, puffed-up toads and half-devoured butterflies . . . this plethora of larvae fills an area devoted in nightmarish fashion entirely to the repetition of the selfsame act: eating, being eaten. Above a horizon blocked by trees, some volcanoes make a show of pointing up to the turbid sky, but it's the insects who lead the dance as they devote themselves shamelessly to their cannibalistic feast. This is the school of Pengosekan (one of whose best painters, in my un-authorised opinion, has to be I Ketut Gelgel) wherein the theme is endlessly repeated, and takes precedence – or so we are taught – over the imagination. And yet, for all their intensity, even the maddest paintings by the Victorian artist Richard Dadd – who, from his confinement in Bedlam, painted a whole population of elves and goblins in a prodigious encumbrance of vegetation – do not attain to the degree of quiet cruelty depicted by this uncelebrated Balinese artist. This hallucination by I Ketut Suparera of a battle between grasshoppers and red ants, whose gnawed carapaces obstruct the view, is deeply disquieting.

Regarding the dream – and the elves and fairies, and the entire fairyland paraphernalia that the English so adore – we must turn to the birth of Hanoman, the white monkey of Ramayana, by I Gusti Made Deblog: a whole bestiary of winged creatures flits through the lianas, each bearing its gift to the infant Hanoman, who was born, as we all know, from a drop of the god Shiva's sperm which his mother, the fair-haired Renjani, accidentally swallowed while she was bathing in a river.

But the most visionary, and also the most seditious, representation of the Balinese myths is by Gusti Nyoman Lempad. In his old age, he had become a living legend. Wasted away, emaciated, polished and hard as old ebony, he died at 116, a venerable old sage, surrounded by his numerous and respectful progeny. On the appropriate day of the Balinese calendar, he summoned his family, had them bathe him and dress him in white, pronounced a few words of exhortation to them, requested that they complete the tasks that his short life had not permitted him to accomplish, then died.

In a strange setting of dead trees, the dragon of lust embraces a huge, long-limbed woman endowed with small wings like a butterfly's, while at her feet, Arjuna, the Don Juan of the Pandawa, who is no bigger than an insect, aims a murderous arrow at her. Like an exotic fruit, a vagina grows amid the roots of the skeletal trees. The spindly limbs, the gigantic size of the woman, the studied disproportion of the bodies, a certain mannerism in the gestures, the line which snakes, undulates, slips in and stretches out, twists into spirals or rears up vertically: Lempad sometimes vaguely resembles Aubrey Beardsley, Wilde's sulphurous acolyte, with humour added – and an erotic freedom.

Do the Balinese dream as they paint, or do they paint in their dreams?

One fine day, the anthropologist Margaret Mead, a redoubtable bluestocking freshly moulded by academia and strongly influenced by Freudian theories, landed on Bali with her erudite companion Bateson, whom she had married on the crossing to the island (the Dutch officials, appalled by her tumultuous love life on New Guinea, had denied them permission to wed in prudish Batavia). Margaret Mead and Bateson were not the type of people to be deceived by appearances. They decided that the Balinese were schizophrenic. Demoniac dances, krises and trances, this was all perfectly explicable as "the return of the repressed": sole responsibility lay with the social norms –

the whole population was cowed by them, so numerous and exacting were they. At one moment excessively good, at the next quite unbridled, the islanders' behaviour could be explained by frustration. It was only a question of proving it. So Margaret Mead invited the Balinese to paint their dreams and visions, and collected these paintings. Word travelled fast in the region: this was a windfall not to be spurned. For a while, the Batuan school (where Mead and her husband were living) were busy exploring the depths of the unconscious, and painted nothing but ghouls, phantoms and vampires, demoniac visions and other chimeras of haunted souls. "A good dream meant more cash. A good dream brought in real money: this consideration no doubt considerably increased the dream potential of the Balinese," so people in Bali today imply. "Who will ever find out whether the Balinese didn't dream their dreams simply to cash them in?" But in the end everyone did cash in, and to this day Balinese schizophrenia has yet to be proven.

The Puri Lukisan is the joint project of the Dutch painter Rudolf Bonnet and Prince Tjokorda Agung Sukawati (whose father, one of the richest men on Bali, possessed – so his son tells us – "some forty-six wives, thirty-five concubines and a horse-drawn carriage", soon replaced by a motor car in deference to progress and to keep up with the colonial overlords). Bonnet settled in Ubud in 1930, in a villa poised on a pond, opposite the prince's palace. Tjokorda Agung was anxious to open Bali to modernity while protecting it from modernity's excesses. Bonnet, with Spies and Lempad, helped him in this by founding the Pita Maha. Among other benefits, this association was supposed to safeguard the painters and their inspiration from the tourists' greed and the temptation to mass-produce. It was necessary to evolve, of course, but at the same time to preserve Bali's particular genius. The galleries ranged along the Ubud road, where the same red or pink parrots, reproduced indefinitely against a green background, are on display, offer the proof, were proof needed, of the difficulty of the enterprise.

Bonnet had the dignified, austere features of an old-time Huguenot. Painters loved, admired and imitated him. During the war he was passed from camp to camp: Parépare, Bolong, Macassar . . . Then, during the 1950s, shortly after Independence, he was expelled from Indonesia (after his alleged refusal to complete a portrait of Sukarno), just when the construction of the Puri Lukisan was beginning according to his plans. So Bonnet went back to Holland, which was Bali's loss. He did, however, return several times to the island, and completed his museum. He died in 1978, but Bali in death is not the end of the matter. The principal act still remained to be played out, one that was, beyond the ups and downs of politics, dedicated to friendship. Upon the death of Tjokorda Agung Sukawati, at a great cremation ceremony – one of the most magnificent ever held – the body of the prince and the ashes of Rudolf Bonnet, brought back from Holland by friends, were incinerated together.

THE LOTUS AND THE "KNALPOT"

A LONG, STEEP STAIRCASE SEPARATES THE MUSEUM FROM the street and the traffic noise. We climbed it slowly: in this sort of heat all movement requires heroism, even if the trees' monstrous size and the parasitic plants entwined around them leads you, like Alice pursuing the white rabbit, ever onwards from one surprise to the next. At the point when you are streaming with sweat and ready to cry for mercy, the ground levels out, the space opens up, and three low houses, half-hidden in the vegetation, appear: the Puri Lukisan. Brightness, all of a sudden. In the middle, a still pool crossed by a little bridge rimmed with small arches, and growing out of it the long stems of pink lotus flowers – here is the seat where Buddha meditates. Add the jet of a fountain, regular and discreet. We sit on the bridge parapet and watch the zigzag flight of the insects, drowse-inducing. Remote from all thought, from all disquiet, from all desire. Nothing counts any longer except this moment in the garden, the broad cup of the lotus flowers and the soft sound of the running water, nothing else matters – nothing else exists. Only the perfection of the shade at the edge of this pool. Even the two small motionless figures are caught up in the picture as though withdrawn from time. "We are eternally there, outside time or change." Rereading the English poet Kathleen Raine, a fervent disciple of Blake, this is how in retrospect I see the two of us, for the moment itself was full – so full that I did not imagine emerging from it.

The protective shade stretched over our visit, over the mysterious and naïve paintings assembled by Bonnet. A third pavilion, at a slight distance from the first two, offered post-cards that two girls were selling. Curiosity seized me – the Bible says that this was Eve's downfall – to look inside. There was a sign with large letters on it reading KNALPOT.

All unsuspecting, in we go. It is a great empty hangar. On the ground in one corner dozens of urine bottles and flashing lights: the work is entitled "Energy"; most of the artists are from Yogyakarta, except two, who are from Bali. From the pink lotus to the urine bottle. I am well aware that the lotus takes its root in the mud and that D. H. Lawrence, champion of the alliance of opposites, wondered at this, but even so . . . Without any preparation, I myself (and maybe Sacha too, astonishment has silenced him) suffer Adam and Eve's sad experience of banishment from the earthly paradise, falling brutally out of the heights of a mythical, eternal world on to the hard ground of History as the twentieth century fashioned it.

The guide, of whom we request an explanation, comes up with two words (perhaps because his English vocabulary is deficient): here it is "modern", there "traditional"; then a third: "It is modern, political."

Knalpot, as I later learned, is Dutch for exhaust pipe: the pipe through which gases and pollution escape. Or again, refusal, revolt, rejection. War against an omnipresent corruption. On the one hand the perennial power of legend and myths, on the other, time resuming its ponderous march, telling a story – right up to date this one – of distress and struggle: the two dimensions coexist, side by side.

On the road to the airport, on the way back (I am running slightly ahead of myself), our driver, an athletic young man in a safari suit, endowed with a sort of grim energy, assured us:

"Our country is going to the dogs."

"Bali too?" (Me, ever hopeful.)

"Bali is part of our country."

"Is Bali being affected economically?"

"The country is affected economically, politically, morally. The influence of the other islands reaches Bali too. Bali is less affected than the others, but things are not going well here either and things cannot go well. In Indonesia there are ten million young people out of work; in Bali we certainly feel the effect of the crisis. This evil has a name: it is corruption. You can say what you will [I had made some timid allusion to certain scandals in France], when it comes to corruption we have you beat."

This last remark had about it a sort of bitter pride that inhibited all comment. Besides, the situation of the country is sufficiently complex and explosive – even if, on Bali, one scarcely perceives it – that it's preferable to add nothing.

At this point we pass a statue of Bima as a child tussling with a dragon. Our driver's pride suddenly shifts focus; his mood improves. "Bima is one of the five Pandawa brothers. You may not know it, but the Pandawa brothers embrace within themselves all the characteristics of the human race: you can think of anyone around you and you will find his prototype in one of the Pandawa brothers. In them there is everything."

Bravo, on Bali the ancient myths are alive and well.

THE BAMBOO CAFÉ

THE EVENING OF THIS VISIT TO THE MUSEUM, WE WANDERED round the dark city streets, still warm from the stifling heat of the day. At far intervals a street lamp shed a little light. At a crossroads a small crowd had gathered around a colossal and indistinct object. We drew near. It was an enormous, obese, clawed monster in papier mâché, shaggy and menacing, with outstretched arms and lowered head, its features melting into the darkness. A dozen men shouting and shoving, pulling on ropes, succeeded bit by bit in hauling it upright. It was now oscillating high above our heads, a giant black silhouette, half-beast half-man, with its hairy mane flowing in the sultry night air. With great effort, this creature of fantasy was introduced into a hangar fairly close by, then it was roped up without ceremony and left in a corner, in anticipation of some feast of the full moon, the following day.

At the restaurant, which we identified by a single lamp, two bearded Americans disguised as rajahs, their foreheads encircled in white, were in quiet conversation, recumbent in an alcove. Their thick hair, swollen with dreadlocks and knotted in pony-tails, fell to their waists. Narcotic atmosphere, whispering shadows, swirls of smoke, dreamy conversation. In the pond beneath the black sky, amid some of the tables, frogs croaked among the lotus. We were brought a spicy rice dish decorated with banana leaves. "Tell you what, two voices in harmony can sometimes carry better than twenty voices in unison." Their discussion floated across to us in the calm of the night.

The people of Ubud recognise them. They go to the temple, mix with the celebrants, take part in the rites of offering. Of the former hippies, they have not kept the distaste for money, but some of the particular habits. Escaping from a materialistic society, from the hard contrast between wealth and poverty, they have come here to play the game of innocence among a popu-lation that is at once tolerant and amused. Bali, this El Dorado of souls who have lost their bearings and are looking for spirit-uality and a new life, has welcomed them. "They are no trouble . . ." we were told.

So they join the stream of painters and artists, visitors who come for a day and are no longer able to leave, held in thrall to a landscape more charged with expression, more vibrant with presences than any other in the world, rooted for the rest of their lives on this island that has a magic, for want of a better word – or, perhaps, the age-old presence of the imaginary – that they have striven to capture. This spirit is diffuse, elusive and yet so manifest that we can well endeavour to paint or describe it, but all the while we know that in the end we will succeed, at best, in transmitting just a whiff of the exotic, that is to say something foreign to our own reality, something veneered and therefore artificial, when what is needed is precisely the opposite: a dimension essential to humanity, a factor long mislaid in the West.

THE DANCE

IT IS ALL VERY WELL TO SAY THAT ANTONIN ARTAUD USED Balinese theatre to contrast it with Western theatre, thus appropriating another culture for his own private purposes of demonstration; he did nonetheless capture, better than any connoisseur or scholar (*pace* Susan Sontag, who credited him with "one of the most seductive fictions ever written about the oriental theatre"), the essence of this art that is founded on pure movement, remote from all psychology, and on a fundamental relationship with fear and hallucination.

Fear – panic terror so uncontrollable, all-pervasive and primeval that its origin is untraceable – is expressed by this masked character with its fixed expression, bulging eyes, mouth pulled into a grimace; it is expressed in his white-gloved hands. Restless, distraught, trembling hands, "hands flitting like insects in the green evening",[1] extended by huge hooked nails, talons, claw, branches even, call them what you will; they quiver and struggle like two frantic birds, flapping in all directions, soon reduced to an intense, feverish, insane palpitation accompanied by the no less insane rhythm of drums and cymbals in the gamelan. The music, moreover, seems born from the movement itself, as if emanating from the spirited bodies of the dancers, the natural outcome of their gestures, so close is the correspondence between sight and hearing, between gesture and sound, "those noises of hollow wood, of sound-boxes, of empty instruments – it would seem as if it is the dancers who produce them with hollow elbows, with hollowed wooden limbs". Bear in mind that the dance and the music evolve on three different planes: the base line, which is regular, the melody, which varies, and the rhythmic beat from the cymbals, gongs and drums, which alone is tied into the movements of the dance. At one moment flowing, at another staccato, the movement may be repetitive to the point of becoming a continuous vibration; add the music, and in no time the effect it has on the spectator is hypnotic: the faculty of judgement is "suspended", vision itself is suspended, inert, one is bewitched, possessed, enraptured, brought to that state that

---

[1] All quotations in this passage are taken from Artaud's *The Theatre and its Double*.

precedes thought and speech, from which the dance seems to issue. "In Balinese theatre one senses a state preceding language and one that may choose its language: music, gestures, movements, words."

Those wild flutterings, those dilated pupils open to some unbearable inner vision, those leaps and shudders, those muscular tensions, they all convey the animal terror arising from the depths, this "solemn hum of everything instinctual", which speech is powerless to explain and which, here, by means of controlled gestures repeated for centuries, is restored to us in a truly magical fashion. In other words, what is implied, given to us to observe and to feel (not to understand), is an obscure and magical reality, with its charge of poetry and terror. That this reality is intimately bound to the world of nature, and indeed to every expanse of the cosmos, is evident to anyone who watches and listens for a moment – this music in which springs well up and insects walk, in which boughs snap and the wind blows through the reeds, these bodies stiffened in a trance, or shaken by spasms, as though preyed on by inner demons or invaded by cosmic impulses . . . It is the island's high volcanoes and its deafening rain, its thick forests resounding with voices that animate the frenzied dance whose stiffness and angularity, whose jerky, fragmented aspect well attests the violence to which those bodies are subjected.

Or this dancer with an ambiguous, mesmerising beauty, decked out in gold like an Egyptian Pharaoh and heavily made up – charcoaled eyes, straight eyebrows, reddened lips in a triangular feline face – whose appearance on stage forces us deeper into a strange sort of limbo. His intensely feminine attitudes suggest seduction, struggle or submission, without his immutable features betraying even the slightest consciousness or emotion. The face is impersonal, as though frozen, nothing moves but the dark pupils in the wide eyes and the head from one side to the other of the neck, as though on a slide. Each gesture of an absolute, mathematical precision, as though ruled from all eternity. These mechanical movements, these eyes that roll madly, this improbable breaking of the joints, these heads that shift from one shoulder to the other, these shuddering motions like those of a marionette whose strings appear to be pulled by some concealed god: all is vested with an exact meaning, a meaning that confers on them the original intention, or the first impulse, and which to us is conveyed in the bodies that evolve before us at this precise moment. Though we may only seize it intuitively, we do not for a moment doubt its force and its truth.

Balinese dance does not seem to represent a story or a situation with the responses it calls forth, not even an emotion, but perhaps simply a state of mind. And this, rendered as by a single gesture indefinitely repeated, reduced to its essential characteristics, stripped bare, purified, until it is an outline that contains and correlates all the differences, this has about it some element of eternity. "A sort of terror grips us when we consider these mechanised beings: neither their joys nor their pains seem to belong to them exclusively, but instead obey rites experienced and as it were dictated by superior intelligences. Ultimately it is this sense of a sovereign and prescriptive Life that most strikes us in this spectacle, similar to a rite that might be profaned."

These dancers, incidentally, are not professionals. In Bali, everybody – butcher, baker and candlestick-maker – is a dancer, just as everybody is a musician from childhood. They materialised one dark, sultry night in the Sukawati palace courtyard. Like wraiths, they suddenly appeared, framed in a recessed doorway, at the top of a high stone staircase. It was the palace gateway, all pink and fairylike in the glow of dozens of lanterns.

As I watched, I felt as if I had crossed a frontier, entered a world of fantastic shapes. The dark silhouette of Rangda, with her luminous halo and criminal hands, blocks the narrow opening of the porch. In the dance of the *telek* a white-masked dancer cannot but recall the knave of hearts in *Alice in Wonderland*, charged with carrying the king's crown on a cushion before the cards swoop down upon Alice in a rage. These frightening creatures inhabit the same reality as I do, unless it is that, *like me*, they are the stuff that dreams are made of. They are not born from art, as they would be on a Western stage, where we remain conscious of the artifice and separation: here is a fairy tale, these elements of fable reveal the ingenuity of the producer. No, they partake of dreams, or of life, which comes to the same thing.

But beyond the magic deriving from the beauty of the architecture of the costumes, music and dance, it is the spiritual dimension, which Artaud so heavily emphasises, that stands out – that of oriental theatre and, generally, of a culture more elaborate and refined than our own; more complete as well, for it incorporates the various aspects of the human person, expressing it in its *entirety*, in a milieu that is not only that of human beings but also of the trees, the animals and plants to which it is bound.

However, it was in Java, at the Dalem Pujokusuman at Yogyakarta, that this "spiritual envelopment" of the slightest gesture struck me most forcefully. This school of classical dance was hidden at the end of a dark alley where rats scuttled through the rubbish, and that evening we – Sacha and I – were the only two spectators. Official, paying spectators, that is, for behind a wooden fence the inhabitants of this quarter of Yogya had assembled, as every night, the children nestled in their parents' arms, everybody watching the production, eyes fixed between the gaps in the boards or, for the taller ones, looking over the top. From time to time a stray dog would pass and he too would take a look and make his comment.

The gamelan players in their red and gold finery, sitting cross-legged on the floor at the back of the stage, had begun to play. Then the dancers entered, walking in a crouching posture, sliding as though along an invisible thread; on their heads they wore strange tiaras shaped like wings, flames or shells, precious scaffolding with antennae quivering on top like the feelers of giant insects. Static profiles, downcast eyes, motionless faces. Then a very slow movement, absolutely controlled and precise to the smallest curve – right to the musical angle of the forearm and hand, to the incredibly curved fingertips, to the tip of the improbably long fingernails. This motion involves the greatest concentration and seems to be dictated from within; imperceptible at first, it spreads through the body – a wave emitted from an invisible centre – stimulates the extremities and seems to pass from one dancer to the next, coursing through them like a single impulse surfaced from the depths, like a single musical pulsation. The result is surprising: while the dance is expressed purely with the body (no facial expression is brought into play), the spirit does not cease to be present and even to dominate.

The utter composure, the solemnity of the spare, linear gestures banishes any idea the spectator may have that some sort of reality is being imitated: it is much more a question of an accomplished religious rite, a rite that breeds the sense of the sacred – even when this dance, performed in front of an audience, has given it a profane character.

That day, like the others, an episode of the *Ramayana* was being staged. Rama finds Sinta once more after a long separation and doubts her fidelity, so Sinta undergoes the ordeal by fire and comes through unharmed, washed free of all accusation. At last the two are reunited. They kneel before each other: only a few minimal alterations in the angle of the joints, a few turns executed with the wrists, carry the story forward, a detour in the heroes' path. And yet, on our Western screens I never saw a dramatic resolution, any scene of reconciliation, that could be compared with the two characters' simple act of kneeling down for its sheer intensity, deriving as it does from the spirit's power of suggestion.

The point is that this gesture is no longer tied to any episode but has come to signify the state of mind it conveys – be it love, jealousy, rage, reconciliation, forgiveness. It becomes a sign, a symbol, and refers not to a given sentiment in its narrowest context but to the essence of this sentiment, this emotion.

And by some incomprehensible sleight of hand this strange, exaggerated, hieratic mode, this bizarre headgear composed of an extravagant combination of pearls, flowers and feathers, these brilliant costumes complete with wings and krises, these postures that leave the body fractured and tormented, they are no longer external to us – what they express now lies *within* us, they speak to us intimately. Identification has taken place.

JAVA

JAKARTA
Cirebon
Bogor
Tegal
Dieng Plateau
Bandung
Magelang
Borobudur
Sukabumi

JAVA

150m

BETWEEN BALI AND JAVA

WHEN IT COMES TO AIR TRAVEL, WE SPEAK READILY OF FLYING carpets, of a magic chest that miraculously links the most diverse lives. We are transported not from one country to another, which is commonplace, but from one planet to another, and the realities thus laid end to end in the blink of an eye have no mutual relationship or common measure, which proves that we are looking at a conjuring trick.

Between Bali and Java this conjurer betrays a notable incompetence – take my word, it is a journey in which each minute seems like an hour. In the tropical sky, gorged with rain like a sponge, the aircraft cabin, which on the ground seemed solid enough, is no better than a plain tin can, paltry debris amid the black clouds, the colossal masses of which open into abysses and pile up to infinity, charged with a menace that is far more terrifying than a crash. After an hour of this regimen between Denpasar and Yogyakarta, you leave the aircraft weak at the knees and no longer very sure of what you left behind or what you hope to find, incapable of connecting life on the ground with the traumatic experience you have just been through. And then you forget, until the next time.

As we left Tjampuhan and its hotel, an American family was making its entrance. Scrubbed, waxed and buffed, bright-eyed and gleaming with health, they wear cowboy hats and the self-assurance of veteran conquerors. Their booming voices invade the lobby; they inspect, organise, decide, take possession of the area whose discreet *genius loci* has vanished without delay. Suitcases and designer luggage are all drawn up in battle order, a long single rank suitably marshalled. The silent little gnome who oversees the allocation of rooms had flashed me the ghost of a smile.

At the Yogya Village Inn we have found his peer, polished, affable, discreet, courteous to a fault, but ready to laugh with us at anything and everything, a word, a gesture, a misunder-standing. This apparent insouciance, this spontaneous merri-ment, the joking response to the most trifling events, which here assume a significance – for laughter binds, albeit fleetingly – this is something we had often noticed in Indonesia; it seemed to us to fit in with the landscape, the free-range animals, the surrounding world, to harmonise with them, like an instinctive reaction of body and spirit. After those hours of bobbing about, it provided the happy assurance of a continuity. Gliding from island to island, this smile smoothed over the disruption of departure. I liked to associate it with what I had recently been reading, with this empire of the Majapahit that crops up in every Javanese chronicle and that will have left this smile as its mark, I imagined, among less important traces, in times long past when the empire yielded under the pressure of Java's young Islamicised kingdoms, and made a mass migration to Bali.

Once outside the door of the hotel, which is not far from the town centre, the silence of the dark night, the still darker shapes of the vegetation that barely stirs, and the intermittent croak of the toads around the pool.

On leaving the airport, we had followed some broad avenues lined with little shops of corrugated iron, avenues teeming in all directions with foolhardy motor scooters roaring through a thick cloud of smoke. Groups of veiled young women strolled along laughing among themselves.

YOGYAKARTA

JAKARTA IS THE METROPOLIS AND PORT OPEN TO ALL THE winds, the "crossroads" where the entire archipelago links Java. Yogyakarta, on the other hand, the last of the princely cities, lying some distance from the coast at the centre of the island, sheltered from the storms that sweep from outside, stands watch over the sum total of a past and over the image of a culture that Indonesia today displays to the world like an alluring poster: it is the Javanese inheritance, old as history and enthralling as a tale.

The *kraton*, the princely palace at Yogya, is its heart; its heartbeat gives life to the province, to the country and to the world all around it. The Javanese hold that space is in effect divided into concentric circles that keep expanding much like the expanding ripples created by a stone tossed into water; in the centre stands the *kraton*, sovereign residence and giant motor of pulsations that command and correlate the sum of human activities.

So that this tissue of space can be even tighter, so that no hollow, emptiness, or solitude can exist – so that Being can be comprehended, assembled, regrouped in its entirety in several broad categories, in accordance with an elaborate system of correspondences that join the most distant realities, the villagers have conceived yet another arrangement: the periphery is divided into four sectors, corresponding to the four cardinal points, but also to a deity apiece, a colour, a metal, a liquid, an animal or a series of letters. To these might be added, if we so desire, a day of the week, and other things besides. For the east, the colour white (silver, coconut milk), for the south, red (copper, blood), for the west, the colour yellow (gold and honey), and black (iron, indigo) for the north, while the centre is an alloy, a blend of colours, the synthesis of the four orientations, or again multicoloured bronze . . .

While pointing out the range of primary colours on the ceiling of a palace at Surabaya the guide crooned: "White is serenity and red anger, yellow is desire and black is envy." He had added a few others of his own invention and made up a little act for the tourists' benefit: "Purple, madam," with a salacious leer, "is lust, and brown, sir," with a conniving glance, "is the wish to kill; blue is sickness, and green, idleness . . ."

The day after our arrival at Yogya we went to the *kraton*, negotiating as best we could the ring walls and the series of courtyards that led to the holy of holies: the central courtyard, or Pelataran, from which one catches a glimpse (no more than that) of the Dalem Prabayasa, the most sacred area of the palace – the sovereign's oratory and the kingdom's treasure chest. Of course, Indonesia proclaimed itself a republic in 1945 and the sultans lost their political power, but a spiritual vision fostered over centuries and reinforced by the Javanese feudal spirit, which contains a good dose of mysticism, is not forgotten in a day, nor even in fifty years, so the *kraton* has remained the heart of the universe, a reservoir of spiritual energy.

In any case, one need only to brave the giant demons who guard it and step into the first enclosure to understand that the clock has been turned back – or been side-stepped rather. Outside, time may continue to flow and human beings to pursue their activities: in here, time has stopped once and for all, one has reached the motionless centre of the world.

It took an old man, striking his drum each half-hour, to remind the *kraton* inhabitants that a little time has elapsed. Sitting cross-legged in the central courtyard and dressed in a traditional brown-and-white sarong, he was reading a Javanese manuscript of the *Mahabharata*. Now and then he consulted an old clock, and, with a single dull stroke, announced the passage of another half-hour – and nothing had changed.

We had observed the effects of time, and the indifference

towards it, when we visited the teahouse in which, beneath a thick velvety coating of dust, green Napoleon III porcelain, huge beer jugs from the Netherlands, tarnished English teapots of silver that once sparkled, are piously preserved: gifts to the sultans by the courts of Europe, souvenirs that bear up well beneath the marks of age which have been allowed to accumulate peacefully.

Or inside the rooms devoted to the life of the Sultan Sri Senko Hamengku IX, the most respected of all, a four-star general in the war of liberation, Vice-President under Suharto, and the Minister of Defence who signed the Independence treaty in 1949. In precious showcases along the walls: a little wooden motor car, its paint flaking off, a riding outfit somewhat the worse for wear, an old washcloth, a harmless pair of socks, the two burners on the makings of a butane stove; then the succession of photos at different ages: baby all swaddled up; Boy Scout among his peers; at school in Holland; after the circumcision ceremony, when his faun-like ears were crowned with the symbol of wisdom; seated with knees apart and a fierce expression for the official picture. Here was a blend of private with public life, and a touch of heroism on display for the masses to worship in the shape of ordinary objects, filed shiny-smooth, worn and threadbare, objects retrieved from time, but with no attempt to attenuate time's marks.

Studied poses, always the same spreading of the knees, the position of the arms and feet, the angle of the head and the direction of the gaze; such were the requirements of punctilious Javanese etiquette – personality effaced, subordinated to the public role. One of the sultans, the eighth, did in fact cheat a little, or so it would seem: here is a Pierrot or dancer with a rose the size of a cabbage planted on his head, an elongated neck and half-closed eyelids, as if hesitating, in his yellowing frame, between arrogance and reverie.

The family tree and its ramified branches wherein flowers represent deceased babies.

Through this palace we ventured, but we had no place in it, no more existence, no more reality than shadows. When we encountered its occupants, they paid us not the slightest attention and we had the strange impression of being invisible, of walking in a different segment of time.

The elderly sentries at the *kraton*, in their dark uniforms with their krises slung from their belts and brown forage caps crammed tightly on their heads, possess an imposing dignity. Their bodies and faces seem to be made of very old wood carved over a long period, chiselled, modelled by pride in their role and their sense of honour. Seated by the monumental gates, perfectly straight-backed, their eyes fixed on the distance, or else crossing the courtyards with their customary step, they never spare us a glance.

But to return to our arrival at the *kraton*. It takes a spot of luck and a firm resolve to get past the outer ramparts, which swarm with people, stalls and shops – whole lanes of boutiques and batik workshops, silverware on display and artists at work. An improvised guide, aided by his mates, manoeuvres tenaciously to retain us. We are harpooned, stopped in our tracks, dragged off, shoved, immobilised, buried beneath a flood of words; no possibility of breaking free. How can one fail to find happiness in all this bric-a-brac, unless one intends to manifest ill will? Which is, our guide is confident, unthinkable. In this damp heat, a surge of energy is always difficult, strength, like ideas, dissolves. Still, one needs quick reflexes if one wishes to escape these merchants' zeal and to discover the second gate in its high stone wall.

To pass beyond the inner wall, to leave behind the clamour of the outside world – this is what the symbolism of the place requires. Then silence, peace, ever deeper as one approaches the centre; the sight of two lordly banyans that symbolise the union of the people with their sovereign. There was a time, it is said, when nobody dared venture within the *waringin*, the sacred area restricted to the sovereign's eye as he sat on his throne in majesty; petitioners dressed in white would come and sit here to await his bidding. All we were seeking was a little shade after escaping from the scrimmage, all we asked for was a little energy to visit the courtyards and reach, with a fresh eye, the central area surrounded by its mystical aura. But it is not a question of the eye, as one soon realises, but of the imagination. There is nothing spectacular about these vast, empty, shady courtyards – these sentry posts, these sheds for cannon, gamelans and open carriages – unless you are alert to the spirit of the place; there is nothing striking about the immense gates separating the quadrangles unless you know that they were erected not to bar intruders but to safeguard powerful spiritual emanations.

We were shown the "Hall of Gold" with its learned inscriptions on the pillars, where the three religions were united – Islam (writing), Buddhism (the lotus) and Hinduism (the giant's teeth); then, at the far end, to the left, the door obstinately shut on mysteries unknown to ordinary mortals. Could it be, as in every place called home, that all there is to see is a majestic bed where the sovereign worshipped the shades of his ancestors and the goddess Sri? It is under the spur of the need to know that our visit ends.

When we came out, a gamelan was playing a slow, sad air – a lover's lament; a woman was singing in a nasal, high-pitched voice, as in Chinese opera. Her tone was so plaintive that, even without understanding the words, it was clear enough that this was a hopeless love.

A little further on in the deserted courtyard, we came upon a dwarf in a conical hat and a chequered sarong. Walking at a brisk pace, with a puckered brow and a self-important air, he took no notice of us – and quite rightly too. He was one of the living wonders that bolster the monarch's energy and effectiveness, along with the albinos, clowns, soothsayers and other storybook characters who pass in procession on high feast days.

THE WAYANG KULIT

I HAD ALWAYS LOVED THOSE MARIONETTES MADE OF FINE leather on a lacy open-work pattern; they reminded me of the leaves I used to play with as a child, tapping them gently to remove the green membrane until only the delicate network of their skeletons remained.

In the beginning there was a tree, in the shape of a leaf, such as children draw. It was pulled from the ground where it was taking root, and here the confrontation began: this tree was at once tree and mountain – in it the two symbols were united – and it represented the equilibrium of the cosmos.

This is, in fact, how the spectacle known as the *wayang kulit* begins: by the display of a tree which the *dalang*, the puppet

147

master, sticks into its base. Then the tree is removed from its banana trunk and the storm erupts. Let two men come to blows, let society come off the rails and the entire universe crack and quiver. The tree is projected on to the screen of the world, the gong booms with violence, making a ghastly racket. Conversely, the ascetic practice of Arjuna, a hero with a hundred weaknesses, will overcome the forces of nature which, like him, tend to get out of hand; the tree returns to its place at the centre of the screen, the gong falls quiet, the gamelan reverts to its regular rhythm . . . Balance is a question, quite simply, of harmony between macrocosm and microcosm. The clear lesson is that men must be careful not to upset nature, which is so easily unhinged, not to disturb the cosmic order, which is more fragile than we might suppose. A little self-control, not too much greed, respect for an internal as well as external order, such are the principles of Javanese education that the *wayang kulit* dispenses night after night across the towns, villages and countryside, as the *dalang* travel the roads with the whole world heaped upon their backs.

The tracks they leave suggest the ubiquity of the *wayang*, who vivifies the same shadows and transmits the same values throughout the entire country, whether in the palace precincts or way out in the rice paddies. It ensures the permanence of the traditions, of a culture shared by everyone, rich and poor alike, townsfolk and peasants. The idea of indirectly using these figures made out of skin, of handling these *shadows*, finely fretted and riddled with light, to represent the drama of living – to embellish it, to set us dreaming, to suggest a mystery deriving from a hidden reality that the visible world reflects – this idea, with its easily deduced philosophical extensions, seems to me typical of the spirit of Java, devoted as it is to metaphysical speculations, to reflections, shadows and echoes.

Those "parchment-shadows" manipulated all night long behind an illuminated screen tell no less than the marvellous story of an ideal society, peopled by archetypes, which is forever razed and reconstituted, an endless flux of positive and negative forces. Of course, it takes a full night before chaos cedes to order: there will be sound and fury, guile, courage and fear, before the restoration of peace; there is the entire panoply of human passions and a thousand incidents all familiar to the audience (for if there are hundreds of different *lakon,* or episodes, the ternary scheme never alters: exposition, battles and cataclysm, entente restored). From nine in the evening till six in the morning, in three acts, three movements, the *dalang* will shape hundreds of destinies and re-establish an ever-precarious stability.

To his left he has stuck the puppets representing the bullies and uncouth characters (*kasar*), for they are needed, such is the way of the world; to his right the more refined heroes (*halus*), who are, incidentally, smaller and lighter, but who will, as everyone knows, defeat their tough but stupid opponents. This might be seen to represent a division between good and evil derivative of moralising Islam, but it is nothing of the sort: both sides are equally necessary for the proper order of things.

Between the one and the other, the *dalang*, whom one periodically observes behind his screen, shakes like the devil himself: he mimes all the characters at once, changes voice and accent, becomes a bleating old crone or a stuttering infant, murmurs and roars by turns, ad libs, breaks loose, quivers like a reed in the wind and all the while remains imperturbably seated, legs crossed.

We were in the Sono Budoyo Museum, which contains some splendid exhibits, but that evening its *wayang* theatre was empty. There was a great stage covered with the gamelan instruments, from the simplest to the most complicated; a projector fixed to the ceiling, the screen partitioning the room into two; a crowd of thin leather cut-outs, in every size and build, giants and dwarves, clowns and princes lying in heaps, pell-mell, one on top of the other; and, on either side of this stage, two rows of empty chairs. A few tourists, intimidated by all this space, slip furtively on to the seats, hesitate, talk together, pass behind the screen, return when the gamelan starts up, then opt for the darker side before changing yet again.

More than Arjuna with his long, delicate features, or Bima the valiant, it is the minor characters, deformed and comical, talkative and wildly gesticulating, who struck me, occupying the screen as they do for a great part of the time: these are the *punokawan*, protagonists of the common people who, unlike the heroic figures drawn from Indian mythology, are a pure product of the Javanese imagination.

Ponderous and slow, lantern-jawed, puffy as a toad, an old witch comes hobbling. Opposite her is a little pot-bellied gnome, looking perplexed; he bustles about, swells up, struts, twists and turns, needles and provokes, returns to the attack like a mosquito; his only weapons are his tiny size and his persistence, but each time he runs up against indifference and each time he mounts a fresh assault. All in vain. It is pathetic and irresistibly funny. The witch remains stone-faced. A few shudders indicate the defeat of the little gnome and his pitiable efforts to assert his existence. Two shadows, one motionless, the other darting about, a fleeting glance, a lowered head, and all is told. A virtuoso performance, mind-boggling; for two hours, we have been hooked by the ballet of these shadows. We discovered later that we were watching the famous clown Semar, whose mere appearance provokes a thrill of pleasure in the audience, and his son Gareng the club-foot. Missing were Bagong, the youngest son, and Petruk, the most mischievous, with his long nose and big lips, who one day had the bad idea of wanting to be king and assumed the pretentious title of Tongtongsot.

Like Shakespearean clowns, the *punokawan* are the only ones who dare speak the truth, to lampoon and criticise the powers that be. Sometimes they go so far that, after 1965, certain *dalang* have landed in jail ... Which shows that the *wayang* has been able to adapt to modern times and its heroes to evolve without losing sight of their original vocation. Arjuna (now rechristened Nusantra Putra) sports a military cap and the latest trend in pistols: he is a revolutionary hero, but still one of the Pandawa brothers. His elder brother Bima is a guerrilla fighting the Dutch occupying forces . . . Current affairs are reviewed, the latest measures are commented upon, for example the price increases and the rising birth rate (the *wayang* touches on family planning as the clown Semar offloads any number of jokes about large families: nothing dissuades like ridicule). The tourists claim their share: a few words in English and the audience thunders with laughter.

During the night people come in to watch, go out again, eat or fall asleep, no matter, they have all been raised on these stories; this is not so much an entertainment as an integral part of their existence, on a par with their other activities, the whole lot blended into one indissoluble whole.

But this evening, at the museum, the spectators are busy taking photographs, perhaps buying one of these leather silhouettes which, in the adjacent workshop, artisans have spent months cutting out and painting in bright colours. The troupe, *dalang* and musicians, have left on their mopeds without even glancing at the tourists who, in the night swarming with people, will somehow find the way back to their hotels with the help of taxis and *becak*.

JAVANESE COURTESY

"WHAT IS TRUE FREEDOM?" KI ADJAR, AN ARISTOCRAT FROM
Yogyakarta who tried to reconcile European and traditional
teaching methods, asked. "It is not the absence of authority, it
is the possession of self-control."[1] While content to explode
from time to time with unspeakable violence and kill some poor
devil, or even several, the Javanese, influenced by the *wayang*
among others, practise a self-discipline that they have elevated
to an *art de vivre*. Of course, not everybody follows the Pandawa

---

[1] Quoted by Denys Lombard, *Le Carrefour javanais*, Vol. I, EHESS,
1990.

and their emulators in their calling to the "science of the within", in their taste for self-control, which involves overcoming one's own self-interest and one's selfish drives while waiting for the detachment that is wisdom; but anybody may devote himself to silence or, if necessary, respond with a smile, a conciliatory smile, to be interpreted however one likes. This will enable one to arrive at a compromise and preserve that famous harmony. No need to rush, just wait, watch, be alert, keep the door open, don't corner the opponent. Then a sibylline response, a compromise. Only an imbecile is incapable of giving way and insists on winning every trick. The fact is, a person does not seek to impress, or to stand out from the rest, or to assert his own opinion and push himself forward – the heroic attitude Prometheus bequeathed us – he tries simply to maintain an inherited position and to fulfil his role as well as possible.

Like the character in Evelyn Waugh's *Scoop*, who would reply "up to a point" when he meant to contradict his boss, the press magnate Lord Copper, and "definitely" when he meant to agree with him, the Javanese take care never to assert too forceful an opinion or to proffer stark truths. A Singaporean ambassador to Indonesia describes in his memoirs how he had brought his Prime Minister, Lee Kuan Yew, to meet Suharto at Jakarta so that they could discuss the role of Singapore as the potential financial centre for South-East Asia. In the course of the conversation, Lee Kuan Yew suggested that Singapore take measures to support Indonesia. Suharto replied, "Yes, yes," which the Prime Minister took to mean that Suharto agreed with him. But, according to the ambassador, all that Suharto had meant was "I hear what you're saying." In his view, the Indonesian President would never accept such a proposal, and, as it turned out, he was right.

The ability to keep one's opinions to oneself is a virtue. Nevertheless, the West has made a virtue of candour – and a vice of "hypocrisy". Let us stop, though, and consider for a moment: complete plain speaking would swiftly transform life into a hell. Imagine a society in which everybody started telling his neighbour exactly what he thought of him (one might play a little game: of whom do we think nothing but good?) . . . Perhaps, after all, it would be better to moderate the idea of candour and alter the proposition from "Let me tell you what I think" to "Let me tell you a [carefully selected] fraction of what I think." The Javanese have grasped the problem perfectly and are less hypocritical than those who praise frankness without ever acknowledging that it simply cannot be put into practice without causing damage.

Another interesting feature of their upbringing: the importance of saving face, keeping up appearances. Instability, tantrums, vacillation and other such flaws, the West is not put off by these displays, indeed it cultivates them when necessary, refines them to the point of constructing a self-image that is entirely acceptable, and even exhibited with a measure of complacency. Think of the stock figure of the grumpy old loudmouth – odious, but in the end a "decent guy". Or the woman who loses her temper and cries at the drop of a hat – her bark is worse than her bite. Such little failings are regarded as signs of vulnerability and thus of humanity, loveable for this very reason. Now in Asia, these domestic eruptions (raised voices, boastfulness, exhibitionism, strident bursts of laughter, explosions and thunderous tempers) not only fail to provoke interest, but are seen to betray a lack of self-discipline and, what is more, a lack of finesse – a major fault, this. The purple face and bulging eyes are to be expected in the "king from overseas", the *raja seberang*, who incarnates vulgarity, indeed barbarity. Showing one's feelings is simply inconceivable unless, of course, one is "a child, a wild animal, a primitive tribesman, mentally handicapped, or a foreigner". At the very least, our manners count for something.

But there is something else in this extreme concern with propriety. The tranquil attitude, the placid expression could be merely the exterior, the envelope of a complex philosophy.

"Courtesy is a tool that allows others, as well as you yourself, to enjoy inner peace." Courtesy works as a means to smooth, erase, iron out our inner asperities which, like fangs, attack, shred, lacerate and hurt; courtesy protects others, and, to some degree, ourselves from any overly aggressive state through which we are passing. And how can we feel at peace while remaining prey to our inner demons when they let loose – or, less gravely, when others' assail us: their emotional fits, their urges, their more or less well-founded anxieties, their frustrations and jealousies, their ill-contained rages and other trivia? ("With whom wilt thou converse? What station / Canst thou choose out, free from infection, / That will not give thee theirs, nor drinke in thine?" wrote John Donne, the seventeenth-century English metaphysical poet who had a taste for paradox; the poem is called "Of our Company in this Life and the Next", and in this "company" he included friends as well as enemies, encouraging the reader to mistrust both equally, right into the next world.)

The struggle with passions and desires, considered the source of troubles and evil, is at the heart of Buddhist philosophy – and it is evident how it still influences Indonesian society. In one of his discourses Buddha says: "Free yourselves of doubts, anger, ill will, hypocrisy, slander, jealousy, greed, guile, deceit, arrogance." Of course. The extreme respect for codes and etiquette is apparently an intermediate stage, one intended for life in society, the outward, highly elaborated aspect of an ideal of excellence.

So the Javanese, like the English, who are wrongly reproached for their skill at dissembling, possess the great wisdom to stifle their inner agitation, to rein in the wicked demons who, at the very least, should remain concealed even if they cannot be entirely eliminated. "Repression!" the attentive reader will cry. "Watch out, danger, the return of the repressed, you risk doing violence to yourself." Possibly, not that anything is that straightforward. To this day the problem remains unresolved, all we can do is state our preferences.

The Indonesian response is never head-on, nor indeed at one remove. Foreigners who have long resided in Indonesia and speak the language fluently sometimes imagine that they understand it; they soon realise, though, that they still have three or four degrees of meaning, if not more, to penetrate, if they really want to see the question from every side.

FROM YOGYAKARTA
TO BOROBUDUR

THE SUN IS SOFTENED BY A THICK LAYER OF FOG, BUT IT IS already a scorching day. Early in the morning, behind a screen of black smoke, we follow the long drawn-out line of lorries. Two-wheelers zigzag and overtake one another in every direction, like buzzing insects. Between the coconut palms and the banana plants, the road makes straight for the white sky.

Borobudur is "the world's largest Buddhist temple and the oldest in South-East Asia"; its approaches are nothing but a tourist factory, the Javanese, who form the majority, on one side, and foreigners on the other, where the prices are higher. Beyond the ticket barriers everyone meets up again. In small groups we skirt vast lawns.

At the turn of a road, the dark, compact mass of Borobudur suddenly comes into view. Imposing and distant, surmounted by its stupa, the temple crowns the top of a hill. The heat is heavy, and, much like pilgrims of old, we walk with our feet dragging but with eyes raised to our goal. As we draw nearer, we discern the pointed tops of numerous stupas that stud the terraces and form something like punctuation marks along the sides. Legend has it that Buddha, in his urge to self-denial, removed his tunic which, as it fell, made a circle at his feet, placed his rice bowl on top of it, then planted his pilgrim's staff atop everything. This is what gave the stupa its shape. In fact, it would seem to be a funeral mound surmounted by a wooden column that symbolises the bond between mortals, the earth and the underworld. In any event, for Westerners, the stupa plainly resembles a bell.

We steel ourselves to tackle the long climb up steep, narrow stairs that negotiate the five terraces and three initiatory circles and lead to the final sphere. It is as well to draw inspiration from the ascension flame carved at the foot of the stairway, or from recent readings about the symbolism of the temple, other-wise we risk skipping the stages and going straight to the goal – puffing and panting even then – and thus missing the kilo-metres of bas-reliefs along the terraces that unravel episodes in Buddha's life, and, worst of all, missing the significance of this climb altogether. In their stone niches, 432 Buddhas smile. Like the Javanese ascetics meditating in their caves, or the gods

dwelling on the slopes of Sumeru, the sacred mountain. By contemplating those hundreds of smiles addressed to the landscape
in its boundlessness, we step into the mindset of the ninth-
century pilgrim: he came there to achieve his spiritual education
and accede to a degree of higher consciousness by confronting
the ten levels of existence. To climb, to rise from one sphere to
the next. The first one is that of daily life: here he would con-
template the regions of desire and damnation, torments and
delights. The second is that of pure forms: he would seek isolation in the galleries, pass through them in one direction, then
in the other, meditating on the bas-reliefs on both sides, following the path of man in search of truth. This journey was
long and arduous – quite apart from the spiritual effort, he had
to walk six kilometres in the torrid heat, sheltered, it is true,
by the shade of the walls, in retreat from the world of which
all he now could see was the sky. Then he reached the full light
of day and the three circular terraces adorned with their open-
work stupas. He would look at the Buddhas seated within. Final
transition. In the last sphere he would find freedom, detachment: the emptiness of the immense stupa at the summit, "closed
on the silence that is deliverance".

Each year thousands of Buddhist priests dressed in long saffron robes flock from all over the world and come in procession by the light of the full moon, bearing their offerings and
their prayers to Borobudur. Like them, we mounted the steps
of the temple. The terraces surrounded by their parapets offered

shade, while the long illustrated strip with rounded and curved figures unrolled at the rhythm of our pace, as did the gentle Buddhas with their changeless smile. The future Buddha was living in a palace among flowers and music, among countless gods who worshipped him, when he took the decision to incarnate himself on earth. In the jungle, Queen Maia slept, fanned by her handmaids; Buddha, in the shape of a stupendous elephant, entered her womb. When she awoke, the queen had dreamt this scene and, thoroughly perturbed, she described it to the king her husband. Then she knew she was pregnant with Buddha and the king left her side and went to live as a hermit.

On emerging from the tunnel of the fourth gallery, the eye can see all the way to the distant horizon. The world suddenly unfolds in a stunning tapestry of light and colours, rice paddies, palm trees, banana plants and, further off, the misty slopes of the volcanoes whose summits are lost in the clouds, and the splendour of green broken down into its every shade, exploding in every form – plumes, tufts, shafts, spears and fans, palms and fringes, as far as the eye can see across the emerald stretch of rice fields. Then all this rich landscape subsides and falls into place, and the austerity of the black rock is set apart from the luxuriance of the scene. This contrast between the Buddhas, erect and imperturbable, in hard, blackened basalt, with their timeless profiles, and the soft background of the vegetation, the extravagant greenery somewhat blurred and softened by the heavy humidity of the air – this contrast rooted me to the spot.

It is all very well to grow accustomed to pictures of the world, to look, albeit distractedly, at the photographs and catalogues that circulate, but one is no less thunderstruck by the complete novelty of certain compositions. This one was totally surprising.

Then on the downhill journey one notices that the statues have been mutilated; several of the Buddhas have been beheaded, such is the frenzied greed of the vendors; all that remains on the bases are the headless torsos.

The tourist/pilgrim, exhausted by two hours of climbing and close scrutiny under the heat of the sun, finally leaves the temple and expects a chance to rest – green lawns to the horizon, freshness and shade at last – but he is in fact only at the beginning of his travails. Little does he know. In the half-hour that follows he is going to experience the worst of that day's trials. The very instant he leaves the temple enclosure, he is surrounded, immobilised, besieged, literally paralysed by the throng of sellers who, unbeknown to him, have spotted him and are patiently waiting for him. They have had all the time – aided by experience – to size him up: degree of fatigue, feebleness of character, decisiveness, propensity to doubt or towards kindness, age, financial means, all this is taken into account; it never takes the tourist long to learn how to assess the salesmen's manifest talents, tenacity and psychological finesse. Initially, he will try to fend them off firmly, then less firmly; in his disarray, he will eventually send his companion an SOS or, for lack of anything better – if he is fenced in – a verbal message. These words, in

whatever tongue they are uttered, do not fall on deaf ears: immediately they are seized on and interpreted, and merely reinvig-
orate the battalion of assailants. Once isolated, the tourist
disappears within the frantic, gesticulating group: he has lost
his support; he sees only arms, hands and objects stuck under
his nose; he hears only a litany, muttered in tones that range
from hectoring to supplication, the murmured confidences that
start with "madam" or "sir", as the case may be, followed by
the mention of a price which slowly drops with the approach
of the barriers to the second enclosure. His desire to escape and
reach the exit as quickly as possible – an illusory desire, since
he can barely move – is compounded with a vague respect for
such shrewd, intelligent determination. This hesitation, this new
nuance in his comportment, will prove his undoing: the assailant,
noting the signs of this climatic change in a split-second and
seeing the nearby gate, will resort to his last and most powerful
weapon – an appeal to compassion. "I have no money," he tells
you with a broad, conniving smile.

And so the shattered visitor winds up with ten coffee spoons
made out of buffalo horn, four statues of Ganesh, a bronze
stupa and divers other items so hideous that he cannot even
make gifts of them. Never mind, he has played his tourist role
as best he might, with no particular elegance or brio, which is
precisely what has been expected of him.

PRAMBANAN

A FEW KILOMETRES EAST OF BOROBUDUR, ON THE ROAD TO
Solo, the small town of Prambanan lies in the middle of a field
of ruins. While the Saïlendra were finishing the building of
Borobudur around the middle of the ninth century, the Hindu
Sanjaya dynasty was constructing the immense complex – some
220 temples and shrines – at Prambanan. Soon after its com-
pletion, it was abandoned just as mysteriously as Borobudur. It
is conceivable that some monstrous volcanic eruption left the
splendid edifices covered in ashes, unifying those regions and
their undertakings beneath a uniform carpet of iron grey upon
which – the better to erase every trace of human and divine
rivalry – a thick vegetation soon grew. Without haste nature

reasserted its rights; for a thousand years the temples lay buried and the cults amalgamated.

Like an apparition risen from nowhere, surrounded by black arrows of flame, six futuristic pyramids stand up against the sky – six spacecraft, perhaps, escaped from the pages of Jules Verne to pose in this alien setting of prairies, pointing towards space, ready to return to it again. Fantastic constructions, works of the boldest imagination. A thousand years earlier, arriving in a thick swarm, they dotted the whole region, which was known as the Javanese El Dorado, with their tall tongues of flame in dark stone. Six survive as witnesses to the invasion, three large and three smaller. Slowly crossing the flat, green stretch, we again have the impression of having left the normal world behind and of reaching another planet: there is no possible point of reference to the familiar sights, to those intrusive thoughts, those spectres and recollections that we drag along with us and that distance us from the place we are observing. At such moments we rediscover something that years and habits have stripped from us: the powerful energy of a first sight and, with it, that sense of novelty that is always accompanied by a touch of euphoria. We laugh readily, the least thing enchants us, even unknown words take us back to our childhood and delight us. As we followed our guide, we marvelled at even his most trivial revelations.

And he certainly had quite a few up his sleeve! He stood at the entrance to the temple among a group of guides in navy blue and white uniforms, all highly polished and full of ardour, and he accosted us with a hopeful smile. He spoke good French and German, he told us; he had learned these languages all by himself, in books, and a little with tourists.

He was a studious young man who spent his leisure hours reading, collecting new words as others collect butterflies; not that he always knew a word's exact definition, but he relished the beauty of the sounds and even their mysteriousness, suspecting a hidden force and levels of meaning too deep to plumb. He adored abstract notions and derived a huge pleasure from abstruse discussions and any amount of splitting hairs. In particular, he had drawn from his manuals of philosophy and history a whole mass of brand-new syllables, precious words like Darwinism, evolution and progress, which he brandished at every opportunity and in every context, and willingly supplemented them, to demonstrate their ambiguity, with words like cloning and euthanasia. A bold conjunction of ancient and modern materials. Where on earth had he fished them out, in some review or magazine? Or on television, which he never mentioned? He had coined or re-appropriated others, Coca-Colonisation, for instance; the sound of these words enraptured him, even though he totally condemned the realities they communicated. After all, before the massacres of 1965, Indonesia was the largest Communist nation in the world outside the Sino-Soviet Bloc, with its million and more adherents, and even today American influence is ill-judged here. The West and its values seemed to him to merit all his mistrust and, without preaching, he did enjoy taking the best-established terms, those that had achieved broad respectability – words like "development" or "optimism"– and turning them inside out like a glove (without, however, realising that these words pose problems for some in the West as well).

He had a heightened sense of the relativity and "ambiva-lence" of things, a train of singing vowels that pleased him and summarised his positions well enough. It was invariably to ambivalence that he returned, for "everything was two-sided" and there was no place for any moral – and thus simple – judge-ment. To be sly, to be a hypocrite? Heavens no, he saw nothing wrong in that, some days it was even necessary, though on others, he would quite as willingly admit, it was to be avoided. Besides, look at Ganesh, god of wisdom and ruse, who was seated there in front of us, replete and at peace, eye half shut and belly bulging: sometimes his trunk was to the right, some-times to the left. The six arms of Durga, wife of Shiva, held a spear and an arrow on one side, a shield on the other. Their functions were not opposed but com-ple-men-tary. According to him, "everything proceeded in binary fashion, in pairs", and our ethics, with their polarity and their hierarchy of good and evil, seemed to him over-simplified and too rigid: good and evil did not exist in isolation, but in constant tension. I do not know whether he was Muslim, as 90 per cent of Indonesians are, but if so it was a brand of Islam strongly tinged with the local spirit.

In any event, Islam is here attenuated by native beliefs which have been implanted in people for centuries and remain confident of their power and endurance; they combine well with the new importation. There is, moreover, the tendency to distinguish the *abangan*, who continue to practise a popular religion beneath an Islamic veneer (and our guide showed all the signs of being an *abangan*), from the *santri*, who espouse a more muscular Islam that assembles the most variegated groups, in a determination to defeat the West.

From one temple to the next, in a heat which smothered any inclination to debate, he persisted in furnishing us with examples of the rightness of his view, finding the positive in the negative and vice versa, showing bodies that were at once female and male, a sun and a moon, they too androgynous – a relativism of differences and principles which appeared to us not inconvenient and more realistic than the cut-and-dried system of oppositions. The sequence of scenes from the *Ramayana* on the bas-reliefs, the rats and the snakes, the monkeys and elephants served for his demonstration as well. Their beauty concerned him less than his own exposition of ideas on morality, which were undeniably not all bad.

It was in the company of this polyglot philosopher that we undertook our tour of Prambanan. "The temples," he informed us, "are built like obelisks, vertically, that is, following the course of erection. But, if you prefer, you may interpret this verticality as an upward thrust." An evident need to reconcile differing

169

orders of reality (but, in the spirit of certain religions, not so much after all). He was now showing us sculptures in the shape of bells, harmoniously swelled in the middle, pulled in at the base and surmounted by a cylinder; somewhat reminiscent of stupas, they adorned the temples in their hundreds – from a distance they produced the flame-like impression that had struck me. In fact, they were fertility symbols, the linga penetrating the yoni, the female organ, but also, for adepts of a more chaste religion, they represented an urge for elevation because, like the entire pyramid, they pointed to the heavens. "In the Christian religion heaven is above and hell below, like good and evil. In Hinduism," which he boldly interpreted without hesitation, "they are on the same level." One might have contradicted him, for do not towers represent the stacking of the worlds that form the cosmos, with a foundation, an intermediate floor and a top, thus a progression? But he clung to his horizontal view, and to get into an argument, in that heat . . . A burst of indignation was enough to knock you over; anyway, I was no longer sure of anything.

When we left him he was still preoccupied with churning out maxims and paradoxes: "Here, we are against Darwinism; we think that the future is in the past, and not simply in the future." Fair enough; at any rate, he cannot be entirely wrong.

PRINCE DIPONEGORO

THE CITY OF YOGYAKARTA IS THE BIRTHPLACE OF THE MOST
renowned rebel in Indonesian history: Prince Diponegoro, who
from 1825 to 1830 fought the Dutch settlers. A small museum,
so well maintained by the army that it remains closed all day,
marks his birthplace in a quiet suburb of Yogya. At Magelang,
formerly a Dutch military garrison, a different museum indicates
the spot where he was taken prisoner and, in the cave of Gua
Tabuhan near Punung, where the gamelan is played on the sta-
lactites, the recess which served as refuge for him can be seen.
Thus the whole of Java is dotted with memorable sites that need
to be connected, like Tom Thumb's pebbles, to retrace this sombre
story of struggle, betrayal and death – one of the all-too-numerous

tragedies which made up this island's past. This one is more complex than the legend would have us believe, because, if the vil-
lain is clearly identified – the Dutch betraying their word – the
hero, a prince stripped of his rights, does have his weak points.

Diponegoro was the eldest son of the Sultan of Yogyakarta.
The English, who played a brief but memorable role[1] in the
colonisation of Java, evidently found he had a bit too much
character and therefore supported a younger person as successor
to the throne. Diponegoro chose exile. From a banal dynastic
quarrel, he made a holy war. He returned a war leader. Like
Joan of Arc, he had received a sign from heaven and he was
going to expel the Dutch from Java. Won over by his charisma,
the people saw in him the legendary Ratu Adil, the "king of
justice" sent by God and announced by the prophets, who would
liberate them from the oppressor. One part of the aristocracy
joined him. For five years they made war, until the day when
the Dutch suggested they negotiate a peace. It was all very well
for Diponegoro to hate them, he still judged them too favourably,
and he accepted their terms. The Dutch then laid a trap for him,
arrested him and banished him to Sulawesi, where for twenty-
six years he was imprisoned in Fort Rotterdam, no doubt
awaiting a deliverance that never came. He was buried there,
in a little graveyard. The rebellion had had its day, an act of

---

[1] After conquering Batavia in 1811, the English were masters of the country
for five years, a period particularly marked by the personality and deci-
sions of Sir Stamford Raffles.

treachery had ended it. A slow decline, tens of thousands of European and Indonesian (mostly Indonesian) deaths, the population of Yogyakarta diminished by half.

In fact, the picture is more complicated than it appears. There is a conflict of forces and temptations – fear, hatred, jealousy, racism – which were only to grow and proliferate. Diponegoro or militant Islam, who was exploiting whom? And what interest did they share, a religion of conquest whose most embattled partisans aimed to establish an Islamic order, and a rebel vociferous in his hatred for the occupiers, who incited his troops to a "holy war"? One hundred and eighty-six "men of religion", these among the most determined, fell in beside him.[1] As for Diponegoro, who liked to dress in Arab fashion with a large white *jubbah* and a turban, he proclaimed himself "the sovereign protector of the true religion". Cleansing the ambient air, sullied by the presence of the foreigner and by the vestigial relics of paganism, was his objective; he would "promote the writ of Islam from one end of Java to the other". So far, so good. Even so, this idea of "true" religion has a stench of fanaticism. The moment a man believes that he possesses the truth, whole and unique, he is potentially dangerous ("A man who is a believer is more dangerous than a ravenous beast," says the Uruguayan writer Onetti). As for the notion of "foreigner", once

---

[1] For further details see Denys Lombard, *Le Carrefour javanais*, Vol. II, EHSS, 1990.

you start defining it . . . Things get worse, in fact, when you discover that Diponegoro was responsible for one of the earliest massacres of Chinese perpetrated by Javanese. One hundred Chinese, an entire community, were put to death by Diponegoro's followers. For nothing. Because they were outsiders, *kafirs*, or invaders. Just like the Dutch, they too were settlers. When things take a turn for the worse, the Other is blamed: the events are construed by a system of interpretation that locates any disagreeable effects in external, and therefore more easily remedied, causes. Moreover, it has the advantage of releasing accumulated anger at little cost. That there are sometimes good reasons underlying an accusation merely complicates the picture a little more, for such a justification blinds us all the more to our true motives. For a long time the Chinese lived on good terms with the Indonesians; the arrival of the Dutch in Batavia in 1619 surreptitiously altered this rapport.

In October 1826, Diponegoro relates in his memoirs, he had a "sinful" affair with a Chinese masseuse. On the following day, he was defeated in the battle of Gowok. The lesson was clear: heaven was punishing him. The conclusion to be drawn was no less clear: from then on, it was forbidden to have sexual relations with a Chinese woman or to take one as a concubine. And since his brother-in-law, Sasradilaga, who had also had a weak spot for Chinese women, was suffering some heavy defeats as well . . . Perhaps more serious than the massacre, a new ideology began to take root with this decree.

Thereafter, the "pogroms" against the Chinese continued. In 1963, starting from the regions of Sidanglaut and Cirebon, the movement spread like a gunpowder trail: Tegal, Slawi, Bandung, Bogor, Sukabumi. In 1966, it started up again with further massacres, resumed at Bandung in 1973, at Solo and Semarang in 1980, to say nothing of the recent riots at Jakarta during which people murdered, raped and pillaged to their heart's content. Shops and whole streets went up in flames; there were gaping holes, blackened façades, twisted metal sheeting, burnt-out carcasses, none of it far from avenues ablaze with colour, with their giant hoardings and the myriad glints from their skyscrapers. Today in the Archipelago the Chinese are what the Jews once were in the West. Envied for their commercial success by the indigenous middle classes, reduced to the position of a "minority" in an essentially Muslim country, oppressed by the government which proclaims its concern for peace but took a series of measures to "assimilate" them by erasing their identity, the Chinese are torn between the desire to flee and the impulse to conceal themselves, by converting to Islam, for instance. But even supposing people are willing to renounce their names, their identities and their beliefs, how are they to alter the features of their face?

IMELDA

THE FIRST TIME WE SAW IMELDA, SHE WAS STANDING AGAINST the black night, her white dress clinging to her very slender frame. She was waiting in the hotel lobby, and as we came in she smiled at us. She had come, she told us, to visit the manager, a friend of hers.

With her dark, slanting eyes, her broad, flat cheekbones and the floppy mass of her black hair, I did find her pretty, but not as much as I was to do. What touched me in particular was the extreme care with which she had dressed, as if to leave no flaw, no defect – this mixture of self-control, assurance and fragility that was evident in her deportment and, when I got to know her better, her laughter and her expression, each telling a slightly different story. She had a Chinese look about her, which was explained, as the manager later informed us, by a paternal grandmother from China; a detail that Imelda, who was not secretive about her family, had omitted.

The following evening, we got acquainted round a table in a little riverside restaurant that she had chosen for us.

That was when she told us her story. Her father was a Christian from Sulawesi who taught theology at the university. Her mother was Muslim and had twice made the pilgrimage to Mecca; each time, her father had accompanied her, remaining, she told us, discreetly in the background. Imelda was proud of this tolerance. But visibly, her mother's calling, acupuncture and its benefits, meant more to her than religious questions: "On the whole they are old men, over sixty, who come to see her, and they all ask her the same thing: they are impotent and they're after young wives. And it works, you know. They all keep coming back. And they're grateful to her . . ."

She herself is barely twenty-five, but she feels old. Old because she is unmarried, because her younger sister is married, and because her mother is anxious. Yet, Imelda has taken care of herself for some years now; she has even been able to buy a small house in an inexpensive quarter and a big car to transport her merchandise. She has started her own shop at Salatiga, craft objects that she designs herself and has local craftsmen execute; she sells them to her associates, an American firm and a Greek one, and next summer, if all goes well, she will open another shop in Yogyakarta. On occasion she is also a model, going regularly to Jakarta to model clothes on the catwalk.

She is brought the sirloin steak she ordered; on the stage, musicians are playing jazz. Imelda has chosen to set the evening under the sign of the West. But we, our heads crammed with images of the day and disregarding her discreet signs, keep telling her of our latest enthusiasms, like the *wayang kulit,* among other marvels. Enough to make her nod off. "That's for the old folk in the villages." Well then (hopefully), what of the Ramayana dances? But she says nothing, no longer bold enough to protest, she is too polite for that, or perhaps she is discouraged. When foreigners, from whom one expects some breath of novelty, start playing the dedicated tourist, the gap is too wide, and the disappointment likewise. She then tells us that it is a question of generations, that the young people follow the traditions when obliged to, but what they actually like is something else, Western music and emancipation. To be emancipated, a hope which her lovers (and she furnishes us with a brief but detailed list, Europeans, Americans, "never Indonesians") have allowed her to glimpse. In this Muslim country where the women are prudes and wait for marriage without a murmur, Imelda, with her flimsy European-style dresses, her high-heeled sandals and her exotic friends, is the rebel and passes for a black sheep. When she stops to talk to a white person in the street, there is always some old crone waiting to call her a trollop.

On the way back, while driving with a slightly reckless virtuosity, she informed us that she liked Europe, the United States, Australia, anywhere but Indonesia, which she wanted to escape. We stopped at a red light and a beggar approached. She talked to us about poverty, about people sleeping in the street, under the bridges, and nobody helping them, about beggars who, after being refused a little change, smashed wing mirrors and windows of cars that had been hard-earned. Her own, for instance, they scratched it one day because she didn't have any small change. Of course this was not India, you never saw people dying of starvation in the gutters, but even so, all this violence, waiting to explode . . . In France, how did we manage? Did we have welfare for the poor? And the freedom to live as you wish, it exists over there, she has been told. If one day she could afford a trip and get over to France, would she be welcomed?

"I too am poor . . . I am poor and have nothing, since I want everything – a career, independence, a man who loves me and sweet children, and a great big house . . . Well, no, I'm only joking, the fact is, I don't want any of that . . ." Nothing. Everything. Between Indonesia, whose traditions she rejects, and the West, which attracts her but which she knows little about – between a rigid society in which she fights her battles without truly belonging and a different society, blown to mythical proportions and ready to offer her, so she imagines, everything that she lacks – she remains of two minds. Look for a place where she belongs, a home base, a reason for stopping there. She is from nowhere, she laughs and scoffs, puts on a brave face, but her eyes are tinged with distress, and in each of her questions we sense an appeal.

RADEN AJENG KARTINI, BETWEEN TWO WORLDS

BEHIND IMELDA AND HER REVOLT, I UNDERSTOOD AS I DUG deeper into Javanese history, there stands a long line of rebellious figures who were wrenched by the necessity of choice – by the attraction of two contrasting cultures, the East, in which they were rooted, and the West, which enticed them. Incapable of reconciling the two, one day these rebels opted for the one or the other, a decision that implied violence to themselves, self-mutilation. The solution to the dilemma may vary, but the price to pay is always the same: isolation. Imelda is pretty, she is brave and she has far-reaching dreams; but an aura of solitude surrounds her.

The Europeans knew how to detect, and take advantage of, this fascination with the West, how to exploit those people who all unwarily served their cause. Such people well illustrated the power of what Europe had to offer and, as Sir Stamford Raffles wrote about the painter Radén Saléh, the tremendous advances that the Javanese character could make under European tutelage. Such was the case of Raden Ajeng Kartini, a woman born in 1879, nearly a century before our Imelda, and indeed one who somewhat prefigured the latter's split personality.

Her father was of the nobility, a *priyayi*, and while still young she learned Dutch. Acquainted, then, with the freedoms (relatively speaking) enjoyed by Western women, she felt all the more stifled in her situation. In letters to her Dutch friends she complained of it bitterly, as also of a culture that was too conformist, in which everything was decided in advance. She dreamt of visiting the Netherlands, a dream that never got further than the dreaming stage. Kartini died in childbirth at twenty-four, after marrying a local ruler and founding a little school for girls. Doomed to obscurity, to futile revolt, to oblivion. But a high Dutch potentate decided otherwise. He determined to profit from this young Javanese woman's enthusiasm and make her a role model. In 1911, he arranged for the publication of her correspondence under the revealing title *From Darkness into the Light*. Darkness characterised the customs and traditions of the Javanese; light, of course, came from the civilising beacon of the West. The book was first published in Dutch, and for a long time the Indonesians paid no attention to it; then in 1938 a new edition, this time in Malay, enjoyed a huge success. Overnight, Kartini became the champion of female emancipation. In 1964, she was elevated to the status of national heroine. Since then, on 21 April each year, everyone commemorates the anniversary of her birth, though there are still some Muslims who object (as they did in 1925 through the press) to her views on marriage and her total incomprehension of Islam. According to the Muslims, Raden Ajeng Kartini was westernised, which was not a minor criticism, nor an exceptional case. Before her, there was the painter Radén Saléh, a still more glorious example of internal exile, whose destiny was as romantic as could be.

RADÉN SALÉH, JAVANESE PRINCE AND PAINTER

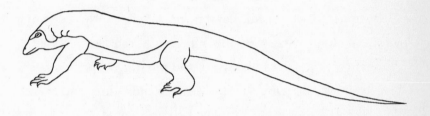

THE CAPTION BENEATH HIS BIG OFFICIAL PORTRAIT READS: "A Javanese prince in the courts of Europe, 1829–1851". Cap on head, drooping moustache and gaunt face, the prince struck a heroic pose. His chest is puffed out, his waist pulled in by a broad belt in which he has slipped a kris, and there is a whole array of medals on his chest; his eye is distant, and he holds himself ramrod straight. But for all this effort to impress, the stance is a little too frail for the required effect, and beneath the martial posture there is a touch of melancholy about him.

In the Bali museum we had seen one of his paintings, the portrait of a Javanese nobleman and his wife, all stiff and starched, and read its description in the catalogue. There was a sober note to the effect that, if the artist had been beguiled by the West, the West had been seduced in its turn as well. Welcomed and lionised by the kings and queens of all the courts of Europe, including Queen Victoria, he encountered the fate of all "cultural converts" so the moralising Balinese author observed: rootlessness and solitude.

Imagine this colourful, flamboyant Javanese prince roaming the German provinces in the nineteenth century, dressed in national costume, mad about art and painting, a penniless student leading a Bohemian life: a strange individual and a complete eccentric, not a type anyone had ever come across before, a person who commanded immediate attention. He spoke six languages and discoursed on the strangest topics. When his small purse gave out, he looked for friends and sponsors. Frederic Augustus II of Saxony offered him protection, then the Grand Duke of Saxe-Coburg-Gotha, then Queen Victoria . . . a triumphal progress. Paris and the revolution of 1848. A voyage to Africa with Horace Vernet. A new taste for animal subjects, like the European painters of the era, and for historical scenes, like the great Romantics. And he painted in oils, systematically, something that no Javanese painter had done hitherto. *Fight with a Lion*, *Tiger Hunt in India*, *The Capture of Prince Diponegoro*, such were his heroic subjects; man was seen grappling with history or with irrational forces, powers that overwhelmed him.

In 1851, he returned to settle in Batavia. Today Radén Saléh

Street, in the Cikini quarter, perpetuates his memory. It was here that on his return he built a Gothic manor to his own design, with gables and a colonnade, inspired by the Germany of Biedermeier, all painted in a gentle pink. And to keep his favourite models in sight, he collected a small zoo in his park. The Comte de Beauvoir came in 1866 to hunt crocodiles in the marshes surrounding Batavia, and en route paid Saléh a visit, which he describes in his *Voyage autour du monde*: "He speaks a little French and excellent German. 'Ah!' he said to us in this latter tongue, 'all I dream about is Europe: it is so dazzling that one has no time to think of death . . .' A singular contrast to listen to this coloured man in his green tunic and red turban, armed with a kris and a palette, speaking in Goethe's language about French art, English beauties, curious recollections of his life in Europe . . ."

It was useless to heap honours on him and invite him every night to the best tables – he could not stop thinking of Europe and its capital cities. In 1875, unable to hold out any longer, he set off again: Florence, Naples, Genoa, Ghent, Baden-Baden, Coburg, Saxony and, last of all, Paris. Then he returned home and no doubt had ample time to think of death. One year after this return, that was his destination.

We did see Imelda once more. We had parted without arranging another meeting. A few questions about our plans, in which she did not include herself, being content to ask about our travels. What conclusion were we to draw from this reticence? Was it typical Javanese discretion, or no interest in seeing us again? Who could say? After floundering in conjectures, eventually we telephoned her. Two hours later, she joined us.

We were to spend the day on the slopes of the volcano, Mount Merapi, a few kilometres from Yogya; she knew a restaurant there in the rice fields. On Sundays the Javanese take their families there to eat, unmindful of the misdeeds of Merapi, which spits out rocks and lava without any warning, crushing hamlets and villages in the process, getting its man without striking a blow. The Javanese do in fact accord the volcano the respect due to power, however capricious and unpredictable it is. They even offer worship to the "mountain of fire" and every year make a solemn procession to the top, where, as a token of homage, a priest deposits clothing and personal effects of the Sultan of Yogya.

Accustomed to living in danger, Imelda drove her car with death-defying bravado. The road was cluttered with vehicles of every description and at every moment we flirted with disaster. But, contrary to expectation, one millimetre short of the fatal collision the car would stop dead in its tracks. At the wheel, Imelda displayed a perfect composure that we were far from sharing. Indeed she would pursue the conversation regardless, visibly oblivious of our vague unease and her repeated exploits. I saw her motionless profile, the fine bone structure of her face, occasionally the broad smile that enlivened her features. This bull-headed quality disconcerted me, those nerves of steel, that serene smile in traffic jams that made those at the Place de l'Étoile in Paris look like child's play – I found it mindboggling. Even as I regularly bumped my nose against the windscreen, I, whom the shortest journey in a car, to say nothing of a plane or a boat, reduces to a nervous wreck, I had to take my hat off to Imelda.

"Do you have enemies," she asked me, "as we have, the Dutch and Japanese?"

I explained to her that two world wars had had no little effect on matters.

That the brief and terrible Japanese occupation was a consequence of the Second World War did not interest Imelda much: after the Dutch, the Japanese, then, after the Japanese, the Dutch again, trying to re-establish a domination already several centuries old . . . whether conqueror or conquered, always the occupier; liberty, independence are words belonging to the realm of dreams. Here, these wars, which took place essentially in Europe and Japan, resemble remote spectacles on television: occurring on the other side of the planet, they assume a somewhat unreal aspect; one does not really feel involved. How odd suddenly to see one's own misfortunes from the viewpoint from which we regard others'. Imelda's innocent question reminded us of our own indifference: most of all she showed us that these tragedies that mark our history and form us are easily overlooked in other parts of the world, erased by sufferings closer to home, or by a past that we know little or nothing about, concerned as we are with understanding our own. It's pointless to mention globalisation, exchange of information and goods, these do not excite emotion or interest, which remains stuck on our own doorstep, inevitably.

By the time we got to the restaurant, it had started to rain. It was midweek and the place was not crowded. A commonplace double-leaf door, the owner's smile, the stretch of rice paddies. We cross the water teeming with fish by means of a network of bamboo walkways that link little thatch-roofed pavilions mounted on piles. A complete village. We continue thus for quite a distance, from platform to platform, until we reach the last one, and then there is nothing by way of horizon beyond the yellow water, the coconut palms outlined against the sky and the clumps of banana plants.

We sit on the floor around a low table. A waitress sets before us the fried fish that we had chosen one by one by pointing at those swimming below our feet. We chat with Imelda, who had brought us photos of her as a model and, as a present, a sample of each item she makes: table mats, baskets woven with exquisite elegance and smelling subtly of grass.

Time stands still. We are poised over the water in this outpost of another world – a calm and lazy liquid world, stretching as far as the eye can see. Our little skiff could drift for hours while the landscape remained unchanged. Here there is neither motion nor threat, nothing but this moment of softness that keeps extending, the flat water surface and the low clouds lost in the same pale colour. And we – we who have found our niche amid these elements as if, in this corner of the world, it had been reserved for us from the beginning of time. It suddenly dawns on us that, on these few inches of bamboo detached from the earth, life is perfect, quite perfect.

The rain starts again, big drops of warm rain that trace lazy circles on the rice paddies. Soon we are surrounded by a moving curtain.

THE *BECAKS*

To begin with we had refused to step into these ponderous crates powered by nothing more than two scrawny shins pedalling like fury. That would have meant going back to the era of litters, or sedan chairs; after all, we were not ailing, we could walk perfectly well. And yet we saw these *becaks*, hundreds of them, all over Yogyakarta, out in the middle of the street, among the buses, the lorries and cars that they seemed not to notice at all; they travelled imperturbably, at the speed of human locomotion, and the locals were glad to use them to cover short distances. Beneath the low hood that protected them from the sun, children would sit, being fetched from school, old women with bundles from the market, men reading newspapers, or sometimes an entire family crammed together as for a group photograph. Once they had completed their journey, the drivers would lie down on the seat with their legs stretched over the side and take a well-deserved rest. In every corner of the city, the *becaks*, with their quota of sleeping drivers, were lined up in the shade of the big trees, though sometimes they were by themselves, drawn up to the pavement in a back street, patiently awaiting a prospective passenger. They formed something like a picturesque art gallery, their panels daubed with lively colours: volcanoes and rice fields, islands and palm trees, little scenes displayed on the sides and back of the crate, sometimes by professional artists, give a naïve or nostalgic account of the scenic attractions from which the rickshaw driver is now excluded. Another less frequent theme of inspiration is the adventures of popular heroes, those of the *wayang kulit* or the *silat*, with blows and battles, order restored, the serial exploits of Javanese Zorros: the *becaks* as a perambulating strip cartoon. Today the authorities have decreed that these vehicles are too slow and impede traffic; they have been buying them up by the hundred, and in Jakarta, where the rickshaws have a hard time, it is becoming difficult to find one. As everywhere else, the motor car is winning.

Despite its modest size, our hotel had its own two or three official *becaks*; their owners would sleep with one eye open and the moment a tourist thrust a cautious nose outside the door, they would dash to offer their services. Over the course of his outings, Sacha had struck up an acquaintance with one of them, a round-faced youngster who would break into open-mouthed laughter at the mere sight of us and who wanted nothing more than to take us in hand: we would climb aboard his *becak*, promise!

And so on the appointed day we boarded, with some reluctance I must admit, one of these antiquated contraptions. The moment we sat down in our small chariot (in which we felt slightly stupid with our knees drawn up to our chin), an animated discussion, which seemed to centre on us, began with another rickshaw driver, who appeared put out by his colleague's luck. Eventually they came to an agreement. With much gesticulating they dragged Sacha off his perch and shoved him towards the other *becak*. We made a half-hearted protest: to be treated like bundles of washing, they could have at least consulted us, since we, after all, were the object of the negotiations . . . ! It was, they felt, a question of money, and they assured us that the fare would remain the same and that they would simply split it between them. This solidarity among people who live from hand to mouth, that was something we noticed in this country, and not only on this occasion. Where do they find the strength to share what little they have? Needless to say, we spent the rest of the afternoon travelling by *becak* and they each received the price of several journeys, which – not to exaggerate our merits – amounted to barely fifty pence per head per journey.

But our two rickshaw drivers are impervious to our

Westerners' amazement; they fling themselves intrepidly, one after the other, beneath the huge wheels of lorries that pound full tilt up the road. This sort of temerity requires, in my view, either a blind trust in the respect accorded to tourists, or the same reliance, this time placed in the dexterity or the rapid reflexes of the motorist making straight for us. In the absence of such faith, we are terrified and moreover asphyxiated by the whirls of inky black smoke coming out of their exhausts. The *becak* bounces and jolts rhythmically, the juggernauts scrape past us with an appalling roar, I navigate on the whole width of the hard seat. Soon, however, the regular jolts of the rickshaw, the sing-song voice of my driver overhead, the sight of the children leaving school in their nice uniforms and smiling at us – all this street-show of which we now form a part, captivates me sufficiently to banish the lurking perils from my mind. My driver explains to me that his colleague has, like him, a family and children to feed, that today he had not yet had a single passenger (tourists are a rarity in these violent times) and that, quite simply, he needs to eat. Wherefore the sharing of the passengers and the fare.

Night falls swiftly, veiling the threatening cloud mass. We pass little stands lit up with a single petrol lamp where people are seated at tables before a bowl of soup; a girl sitting on the ground uses her fingers, on which she has put plastic gloves, to eat a little rice laid on a banana leaf. On the road the lorries continue to thunder past.

CONTRASTS

Once again I am jumping ahead simply to shed light on certain contrasts, much as two pictures might be juxtaposed for the sake of comparison. These contrasts are, in any case, more apparent in the towns than in the countryside, and they do not require any commentary.

In Jakarta, my brother, anxious to introduce us to various facets of the city, took us to dinner at the Grand Hyatt hotel. A son-in-law of Suharto was one of the hotel's principal shareholders. We entered the lobby, where everything is designed to impress. Luxury, grandeur, but never to excess. Each line, each detail conspires to the general effect: the staircase of unnecessary width bordered by escalators, the vast gallery on to which it gives and where fine maples are symmetrically planted, the water flowing abundantly over fake rocks on either side of the steps and the fountain spurting up superbly in the middle of this monumental ensemble. Roomy lifts, silent as tombs, waft us up to the upper floors. On the fifth floor we come out on to one of the roofs. There are several bars up there next to a tropical garden with trees and foliage opening to disclose a pool of green water. People are reclining on deckchairs, from time to time sipping fruit juice, the only action permitted by the heat and the sense of well-being. Around the tables, pretty girls who look as hard as nails are ogling a few obese white businessmen; they throw a lazy glance in the direction of the latest arrival. The waiter brings us a spicy rice dish mixed with indiscernible scraps of meat, the *nasi goreng*.

Down below, in front of the entrance, the traffic flow continues; upon arrival, one has only to hand one's car key to the doorman; upon departure, one has only to get into the vehicle which he will have parked, then brought back. Dressed up like an idol, a distinguished Javanese lady stands tall and waits without moving a muscle, head erect, gaze lost in the distance.

THE BROMO

LEAVING YOGYAKARTA WITH REGRET, WE CROSSED JAVA BY TRAIN
as far as Surabaya, a compulsory stop for anyone wishing to see
the smoke rising from Bromo, the island's most famous volcano.
Javanese trains would horrify those drivers who cannot set out
on a long weekend without listening to the recommendations of
the public authorities about making sure to fasten their seat belts.
The wide doors of the carriages are flung open, and a thicket of
bare legs and arms protrudes; the travellers all enjoy the coolness
and the slipstream, blocking the exits where they perch, half in
half out, in a serene equilibrium. The carriages rattle along at
high speed in an infernal clatter. We notice the crammed corridors, people standing, human clusters clinging to the doors.

In our train, pompously named the Executive, we have been jolting along peacefully for hours, daydreaming before the passing scenery. Tea plantations, rice paddies dried out after the harvest, pale stretches sown with heaps of black and still-smoking grass. A few herds of goats wander in semi-liberty, watched by a herdsman squatting beneath his straw hat. Villages can be seen, crouched beneath the trees, their roofs making broad splashes of russet colour. On the horizon, the mountains roll away into the mist.

After Pasuruan, a town some half a day's drive from Surabaya, the road suddenly climbs; in the space of a few bends one is more than two thousand metres higher up and in an enchanted land. It is not only that the vegetation has changed or that the air is lighter – nothing out of the ordinary about that – it is a phenomenon that anyone may have experienced up in the mountains.

The volcano and the Tengger, the people who dwell on its slopes, have long been cut off from the rest of the world; they are isolated because there are no roads, but even more so by the awareness of belonging to the sacred universe of the mountain, of rubbing shoulders with the gods, a neighbourly relationship that naturally makes them a rather special people. Warmly clad in layers of shawls, they get about on horseback, looking ferocious as they tower over the tourists; these are today venturing boldly across the sea of sand in their four-wheel drives, right to the foot of the crater whose 246 steps they slowly climb like an unbroken column of ants. All-conquering Islam has no hold on this enclave, secure in its privileged position; here the ancient cult of nature is celebrated. As among the Hindus of Bali, small altars in the shape of seats set on high plinths await, at the bend in the road or in the village squares, the visit of the spirits of earth and air. Once a year, on the feast of Kesodo, the Tengger climb in a great procession to the summit of the volcano, where they throw their offerings into the spirals of smoke: goats, fowl and other domestic staples appreciated by the gods, but no longer, as once upon a time, human beings. Legend has it that an ancestor of the Tengger, Kyai Dadaputih, who lived with his wife in the most abject poverty, offered a prayer to Mount Mahameru. The answer came back to Dadaputih that he would enjoy abundance for ever after – white and red onions in profusion – if he consented to sacrifice his youngest-born to the god of the volcano. The vegetables grew. But Dadaputih and his wife never got around to honouring their debt. Threatened with a catastrophe, they one day had to resign themselves to throwing their youngest son into the abyss of Bromo; he was their twenty-fifth child, and one version of the legend suggests that the affliction the couple were spared was not so much poverty as sterility. The statue of Dadaputih and his wife feature in a prominent position at the entrance to the village on the road to Bromo, and their memory is venerated as is that of Abraham who, according to the Bible, likewise agreed to sacrifice his son Isaac to the Lord. It should be added that in both cases the child was saved.

A few days before this excursion we had been to the geographical centre of Java to view the crater of Sikidang, near the Dieng plateau; it was less majestic than Bromo's crater, and on a smaller scale, but this allowed us a closer approach. An infernal bubbling at the bottom of a giant cauldron. Black mud projected in clots, thick and shiny as beach pebbles, a sequence of strange action sculptures that leap and dance amid the sulphurous vapour – jets, dots, blots, accumulations, shredded tatters, motifs in polished metal flung into the air by a formidable energy, only to fall back the next moment. An outpouring, a perpetual re-invention, the source is inexhaustible. One stops there, mesmerised. And suddenly the wind changes; enveloped in a nauseating black cloud, already half asphyxiated, we have no choice but to beat a hasty retreat.

In its magnificence Bromo takes no notice of this furious agitation. The smoke, slow and calm, now white and light, now denser and thickened with grey, a regular breathing – the ample respiration of the earth. Measureless in its power when it is drawn from its tranquil slumber, it can in a few hours change the face of things: the locals, who are not interested in reasoned explanations, have made a god of it. We were perched on our mountain ridge looking at the upper slopes that broke in circles of mist, the largely flared summit emerging beyond, as though floating above the clouds, and the puffs of pale steam rising into the silent air of the evening. Before this prodigious presence, the world of trivia was, as it were, abolished. I spent a good hour motionless in what was soon a biting cold, dumb-struck by this landscape, subscribing unreservedly to the Tenggers' interpretation.

Today in the West we belong to a civilisation where every-thing is measured, quantified, standardised, whatever it may be, endowed with a scientific explanation that recognises the origin and limits of given phenomena. As research becomes ever more precise, not even volcanoes and their eruptions lie beyond the reach of graph curves and calculations, or escape being cut down to size. We should not, of course, regret the discoveries of sci-ence, nor the progress of technology; if we go to the heart of the matter, what we must ponder is rather the way in which science and technology have influenced, not to say determined, our conception of the universe and our place within it. Regulation, "calculability" of existence – we are even insulated from the cosmic uncertainties, and content to be surprised by the occasional storm, which we are then quick to attribute to our poor management of the planet.

But, in our urge to dominate the world, have we not suc-ceeded merely in adjusting the walls of our prison, depriving ourselves of a dialogue and of a measuring scale that raised us beyond our normal frontiers and confronted us with the inten-sity of our desires? A correspondence between various orders of immensity that are perhaps not mutually unacquainted. This at least is the idea that occurs to you as you consider the volcano Bromo, this colossal natural spectacle, and you are reminded of other dimensions, you call to mind a harmony extraneous to mankind, the one that the Balinese strive to preserve with their offerings and their ceaseless observation of the countryside.

Whether it is the imagination or the sense of the sacred that is heightened, as we watch this spiral that slowly rises from the centre of the earth, we abandon the usual points of reference. Then it matters little what it is that is reborn in us – the desire for otherness, the need to breach the boundaries, or maybe the primeval religious awe stirred when something transcends our understanding – since this vision confronts us with the loss of every norm, every measurement, and returns us to boundless space.

Some fifty metres below our observation post is a desert of lava as smooth and bare as the palm of one's hand. All about, at right angles, the wall formed by the ramparts of this ancient crater rises; in the distance, to the south, the hills stretch away as far as Mount Mahameru. Step after step, those who choose to tackle the place find their way down the flank of the cliff. Then, to cross the lunar surface, they mount a donkey or a horse and carry on, patiently, amid the small whirls of dust; for those who view this landscape of death from above, the riders are reduced to simple black dots crossing the grey immensity. They disappear into the distance and are soon barely visible, these pilgrims to Bromo, the mythical mountain.

IN SEARCH OF RIMBAUD

THE NINETEENTH CENTURY WAS HAPPY TO EVOKE THE "Oriental mirage", a mixture of awe and fascination, corsairs, pirates, slaves, unheard-of splendours and unexampled cruelties, and the jungle where uncontrollable forces prowled, those of instinct in the pure state. To the fevered imagination of the West sickened by, or in any event thoroughly uncomfortable with its civilisation, the Orient was a reservoir of myths and dreams – of marvels and perils interlaced. No doubt the shadowy spectres it raised did in fact surface from secret and unfathomable depths, from a pit in which passions fermented that were best ignored or repressed (as in Henry James's *The Beast in the Jungle*); it were as well to leave one's thoughts to wander and come up with visions, with beautiful and terrifying visions by way of compensation.

I don't know whether this idea of the East has been nurtured by stories, poems, departures and yearnings, and engraved on my memory in the course of my reading, but the very word Java works on an area of my mind which might be called a hankering for otherness, or for escape, acting as a powerful stimulus. "Java." The effect is miraculous. Something like that of Ali Baba's "Open Sesame!": reality opens up a chink, an escape path appears, an opening, a passage towards the infinite. Java is a good deal more than a journey, a country to discover or a reality to explore: it is a departure into the imaginary, an incursion into the land of poetry.

Such poetry could in my view only be translated in the evocation of the romantic and tragic lives that assort with the history of this island – lives whose brief span traces a path of light: those of Walter Spies, of Diponegoro or the painter Radén Saléh, and, even more, of Rimbaud, who enlisted in the East Indian Army, arrived at the heart of Java, at the foot of the volcano Merapi, then fled back to Europe.

I am not surprised that Rimbaud, then just turned twenty-two, embarked, one April day in 1876, for Indonesia, a mysterious voyage that his biographers have not dwelt on, preferring the Harrar, where he stayed for a longer period; some biographers have even dismissed the trip to Indonesia as a "curious escapade". First his adolescent flits, writes Alain Borer, a kindred spirit who followed in his footsteps (*Un sieur Rimbaud*), then escape. "The sorties around Charleville, then to Paris and Douai, then to Belgium and England, the trips all over Europe and out to Java" were so many rehearsals for the great African escapade. Java, a dry run.

Early one spring morning in Paris, soon after my return from Indonesia, I went to the Maison de l'Asie to look up the *Bulletin de la Société des études indochinoises*. It reprints the lecture given by Louis-Charles Damais at the Centre culturel français at Jakarta in 1956. Its title is "Arthur Rimbaud in Java".

The Maison de l'Asie is housed in a quiet, well-appointed nineteenth-century building with nothing to distinguish it from others lining Avenue du Président-Wilson except for a discreet engraved copper plaque. Entering the building gives you the sense of retreat – as if the street and its traffic faded out behind you. The confined universe of the library, with its empty tables and magazines sent from overseas, closes round you and your inner adventure like a protective bubble. It was there, among respectable Parisians, that I was going to pursue the search begun in Java one exhausting afternoon devoted to walking and waiting – and on that day I was given a small taste of life as experienced by Rimbaud. On arrival, I handed in a slip – no need to call anything up on the computer – and in a moment a smiling young woman gave me the precious little document sent from Saigon.

M. Damais bases his study on an article by a certain

M. Van Dam, a specialist in historical research who was such a stickler for precision that he devoted an entire article, written in 1942, to the slang used by troops in the East Indian Army. In order to follow Rimbaud, he sifted through a whole mound of official documents, notably the military archives. He nevertheless advanced the questionable theory that Rimbaud might have submitted to the lure of the "oriental mirage", of which he had no doubt heard "in the course of his ceaseless excursions, particularly to Antwerp, or perhaps Marseilles, where he worked as a docker". Apart from that, little in the way of private comment, which is all the better; simply an accumulation of details that, in its very dryness, gives one pause.

The Royal Army of the Dutch East Indies, as it was called at the time, was – M. Damais establishes at the outset – a veritable Foreign Legion. Van Dam, whom he clearly admires, had resorted to a little game with numbers, counting up year by year the nationalities composing this army and the number of recruits per nation: more than three thousand Frenchmen in a few years. Given the statistics, it is not absurd to imagine that Rimbaud, who had been rubbing shoulders in all manner of circles, may have met one or several of these desperate characters and decided to follow them – another of Van Dam's hypotheses.

At all events, what is certain is that Rimbaud reported to Haderwijk, the recruiting depot for the East Indian Army, on 18 May 1876: "He is recorded in the archives of the said depot as having on that day been 'taken on the strength of the contingent'." The next day he signed on "as soldier for six years running from the day of embarkation with a recruitment bonus of 300 florins". There follows a minute description of camp life for the new recruit, who was required to put on his uniform and listen to a reading of the military code before receiving, several days later, the bulk of the coveted emolument. Van Dam remarks that Rimbaud, who was so often penniless, must have regarded such a sum – the equivalent of six hundred gold francs – as a fortune, but that "he would probably have squandered most of it celebrating with his new comrades". This third hypothesis is even more dubious than the two earlier ones.

The task assigned to the mercenaries was to subdue a revolt among the Aceh. The Aceh lived in the extreme north-west of Sumatra, and actively resisted the Dutch. Then, in 1873, the Dutch declared war on them. Ten thousand men deployed, bloody battles, the sultan defeated, the capital taken. The Aceh did not admit defeat, however; they launched a guerrilla war in all directions under the banner of a "holy war". Such was the situation when Rimbaud signed up.

The day came to set out for Java, whereupon the soldiers received a different uniform in blue serge with blue frogging and a grey overcoat for travelling, along with a high kepi trimmed with an orange braid. (It seems that, as in good society, each new occasion in a soldier's life required a change of attire, something to do with decorum, with image, with respect for the role.) On reaching the Red Sea, yet another costume change, tropical kit this time: white canvas tunic (like that worn by house painters), blue-and-white striped trousers, Scots tam o'shanter. Given the unbearable heat in those parts, it is hardly surprising that some recruits already wanted to pull out.

In fact, the moment the soldiers received their bonus, observes M. Damais, they felt their zeal abating, for "how many came back from the East after six or ten years' service?" The choice between a slow demise from fever and a quick death: sickness, a stray bullet, the natives' wrath. The authorities were well aware of this and took every precaution to prevent the troops from escaping. On the morning of embarkation, the soldiers had formed a column to proceed to the station, hemmed in by a strong detachment of guards with fixed bayonets; and at each port, British police patrolled the quayside, to say nothing of the guards on board. But on 11 June, Rifleman Marais, born in Paris in 1847, jumped overboard. The reasons for his act were not understood. "He could not be recovered from the water and will therefore have drowned." After Naples, where they were furious at not being allowed ashore, some riflemen of Italian origin tried their luck on the Suez Canal; on 28 June, 1876 seven of them disappeared, and only one was recovered – he was shipped out on the following vessel and, once landed in Java, he made off for good. On 2 July, another rifleman leapt overboard into the Red Sea; he was never found. (Another one did likewise in Sumatra later that month as the *Prins van Oranje* was docking at Padang, but this one was fished out.)

In any event, on 10 June 1876, the steamer *Prins van Oranje*, of the Netherlands Steamship Company, sailed from the port of Den Helder in Holland. "The soldiers had their hammocks in the hold reserved for the rank and file, and were given a week's ration of coffee, tea, sugar, butter and biscuits. Southampton was the first port of call, where provisions and livestock for slaughter were taken on board." After leaving Southampton, Rimbaud received in addition a packet of tobacco (for smoking and chewing) and a wooden pipe; moreover, games had been distributed among the recruits so they could play lotto and draughts. Six weeks passed in this way, disrupted by suicides and escapes.

On 22 July, they arrived on the roads off Batavia. The troops, boosted by a ration of fresh white bread and a glass of wine apiece, were transported by special tram to the Meester Cornelis barracks. "The look of these new barracks, which until 1848 had been a tea processing plant, could not have been all that inviting."

Rimbaud had been logged into the register with a number of identifying details. These included: distinguishing marks: nil; height: 1.77 Dutch cubits.

Then the "left flank half battalion" was ordered to Salatiga. The route took them through Semarang on the north coast, which they reached by boat. M. Damais thinks that Rimbaud embarked on the *Minister Fransen Van de Putte* on 30 July (a pity that a more recent biographer gives the ship the less intriguing name of *Pakar Ikan*). At Semarang they took a forty-five kilometre train journey towards Solo, alighting at Tuntang. Two hours' march through the jungle brought them to the barracks at Salatiga.

Now the military training began.

A few days later, on 3 August, his companion Michaudeau, who had also been posted to the first infantry battalion, died. A few days later still, on 15 August, not three weeks since his arrival, Rimbaud missed roll call; the previous day he had registered to attend the Mass of the Assumption.

Van Dam thinks that Rimbaud had never contemplated leading a soldier's life, that getting to Java had been his only goal and that, as soon as he had attained this goal, he thought only of escaping.

A goal? To reach Java? Van Dam's interpretation could be hazardous. What does Rimbaud say? "In fact the chances are one will go where one does not want to go, do what one would rather not do, and live and die in not at all the way one ever had in mind, without the smallest hope of compensation."

And as for his enlistment: "His plans to enlist in the Spanish, Dutch, American army," observes Alain Borer's biography, "like so many uniforms dreamed up in order to identify with his father even to the point of desertion, these could not and would not lead him to anything but failure."

Rimbaud was never found, and four weeks after his disappearance, on 12 September 1876, he was struck off as a

deserter, in compliance with regulations. In such cases the delin-
quent's possessions were auctioned off. An inventory was made
of Rimbaud's, and the yield, including two forage caps, a pair
of European shoes and a towel, amounted to 1.81 florins.

"Rimbaud having incurred, according to the record, no debt
to the state, and leaving no known descendant, legitimate or
illegitimate, the total proceeds from the sale were paid into the
public purse at Semarang . . . via that of Salatiga."

All trace of Rimbaud's passage through Java was erased.
"Tracks lead to the body . . . Rimbaud's tracks are fascinating
because they point to a body beyond recovery."[1] No body, then,
not a sign of one. "So here is Rimbaud – on the run. Rimbaud
is forever on the run, clearing off! . . . He keeps vanishing at
the first sighting."

He threaded his way through the stifling heat of the jungle,
through creepers and enormous trees, for the fifty or so kilometres separating him from Samarang. "I am a footslogger,
nothing more than that." He boarded the *Wandering Chief* en
route for Ireland (a ship visibly earmarked for him, though M.
Damais had not yet learnt of its name), endured a terrifying
storm off the African coast south of Durban, docked at St Helena
where the vessel was repaired, then Ascension, the Azores,
Queenstown, Cork . . . then Liverpool, Le Havre, Paris, where
he was seen out and about dressed as an English sailor, and

---

[1] This and the following quotations are from Alain Borer, op. cit.

finally, as always, Charleville. But scarcely had he arrived than he was off again.

"The elemental Rimbaud question . . . is not the illusory one of a discontinuity in his life; it relates rather to the permanence of renunciation, the repetition of self-denial, the passion for defeat."

We had returned to Yogyakarta, not far from Semarang, and here was a great temptation to set off again in Rimbaud's footsteps. In his biography, Borer lists those who felt this urge, and who yielded to it: some dozen books are the outcome, always bearing the same title: *In the Steps of Rimbaud*. To go in search of the poet "is to join these writers' caravanserai". So be it. But this time it was all a matter of locating a barracks lost in the heart of Java.

So it was that one grey morning we set out for Mataram, on the way to Solo, then Salatiga. Our driver's name was Kusuma, and his English was fluent – a stroke of luck because, as it turned out, he spent more time as our interpreter than as driver. With his round eyes, his animated face and his perpetual smile, he reminded us of those Balinese masks made to express positive forces. It was thanks no doubt to this genial fellow that we obtained the unexpected assistance of the army, which was generally reputed to be unaccommodating. By the end of the trip he was hooked on this mysterious M. Rimbaud who had been dead for ages, and whom we were tracking with such bizarre determination; or perhaps this hunt for the vanished poet struck him as a game both diverting and novel. Whatever the case, his assistance was unflagging.

From Solo to Semarang we crossed the middle of Java. Chequerboard of rice fields, narrow rims of land ruled with a straight edge, steeply climbing terraces. And the banana and papaya plantations. The crowns of heavy green fruit around the slender trunks beneath the plume of leaves. We passed through towns and villages, greeted each time by the compact swarm of two-wheelers, helmeted insects with steel eyes advancing like an invincible army, mighty in their numbers and in the racket of their motors. The road had been climbing for an hour or so – we were on the slopes of a volcano.

Once a Dutch garrison post, today Salatiga is a peaceful little market town where the Javanese come for the weekend to escape the heat. Beyond the market, which was in full swing, the main street makes a hairpin bend and continues up the hillside. Kusuma had sought directions to the barracks, and we were sent to the upper section of the road. We passed little colonial houses, neat and elegant, with their pillared porticoes and their gardens planted with palm trees. So what Rimbaud beheld at the end of his odyssey was this static setting, not so different from what I was now looking at: a tropical suburb, nothing more than that, slim pickings for the imagination. On the other side of the road, the somewhat taller official buildings lined up, pompous and massive as they would have been from the start; now they all bear the name of Diponegoro. We stopped at the largest. It was surrounded with grilles and barriers, swarming with armed troops marching in the courtyard, as unwelcoming as could be. Entrusted with a preliminary question, Kusuma advanced towards them; to see the ferocious scowl that greeted him, we had to admire his courage. "Were these the barracks?" "All these buildings were barracks," was the answer he brought us, looking bemused.

Was it at this point or a little later, after two false starts, the same useless wait each time, the same confused explanations across a vacuous bewilderment, that we understood the truth and the scope of the disaster?

The whole of the upper town was covered in barracks: up here, the army headquarters, down below, the headquarters of the military police, to whom we were of course directed for more information . . . Thus began our long quest, punctuated by lengthy stops, by aborted attempts, full of hope to begin with, more hesitant later on, absurd dialogues and moments of heroism.

At the far end of a long lawn, in the shade of a banyan, the police were in a circle, chatting. This time we stuck with Kusuma, who translated our questions. Here were these whites cropping up out of the blue, looking for a French poet who died in the nineteenth century. Not exactly something that happens every day. A plaque commemorating him, maybe? Further policemen, informed of the novelty, came running up from every side; everybody got involved. Did they recognise the name Rimbaud?

Negative answers. An old man, whose teeth wobbled with every word he spoke, took the situation in hand: there was a plaque on a hut inside one of the barracks. It was the oldest in the town and by far the biggest, we would have a good chance of finding some trace of our poet there. He pointed us some kilometres further off, to the top of a hill.

On our left the barracks overlooked the road: a row of identical hutments surrounded by barbed wire, on a green meadow open to the sky. Barriers down, guards looking haughty and suspicious, dressed in combat boots and camouflage fatigues. We had to leave our passports at the gate. In the little guardroom the television was on, a fuzzy picture, animated cartoons which the soldiers were watching to pass the time. Boredom. Rimbaud's own was bottomless and clung to him body and soul. His words came back to me: *"I get terribly bored, the whole time; I've never even met a person who gets as bored as I do."*

I wrote down the object of my quest in large letters on a white sheet of paper: RIMBAUD, followed by a date, 1876, and handed it to the officer who came in at this point. He does in fact know the plaque, but no longer recalls the exact wording of the inscription. We are ordered to wait, he would go himself with Kusuma. An hour passes, the television screen flickers, Tom and Jerry play cat and mouse, soldiers appear at the window and give us a curious glance as they move on. We feel we have been there for ever, in this hut set down on a hilltop, in this empty landscape in which Rimbaud, armed with his rifle, is preparing for flight. Time stretches out, we shall never get away; our search remains open-ended, with no resolution possible, just like our absurd questions, our indefinite wait, like the echo of a name that resounds and rebounds without a response. Eventually the two enquirers return. The plaque they read did not bear the name of Rimbaud. We had already made up our mind, this was the way things had to be. The officer, who was by now caught up in the game, rang the military headquarters and explained our request; the commander-in-chief would see us. Equipped with our sheet of paper and the name Rimbaud, we set off again.

Another guardroom, its walls as bare as the first, but crammed with soldiers and telephones. My sheet passes from hand to hand. They read it in perplexity: Rimbao. Rimbao, they repeat as though for a question, the voice trailing on the o's. The senior officer is called while the telephones ring and information flows in. The chase, begun in 1876 in this very place, when Rimbaud set off on foot down the road to Semarang, resumes more than a hundred years later. Time has stood still. Rimbaud has just escaped, he is hiding in the jungle a few kilometres from here. The entire army checks it out and pursues him. Rim-ba-o, one hears on every side; but all in vain, Rimbaud is unknown, elusive. The senior officer arrives, a man with a sharp profile and an inquisitorial eye, who takes a serious look into this story of a poet gone to ground more than a hundred years ago in the heart of the jungle. Another plaque is hunted, another clue followed, the wait starts all over (with no better result than the first time). "Did these barracks exist at the end of the nineteenth century?" No, everything was torn down and rebuilt in the interim. The weather attacks stone, eats away at houses, everything disintegrates, falls to pieces, keeps crumbling away, returns to nothingness. The buildings disappear and with them the chances of an indicative sign. But have the barracks always been here at least, in this part of town? Yes, always, same spot, different buildings. Which leaves this bit of hill, a bare line against the horizon.

The thought of recovering the traces of Rimbaud proves illusory. The barracks in which he briefly stopped have been carried away by the wind and the rain, nothing lingers in memory, no tribute to a name only vaguely noted, not even a false trail like the fictitious house in the Harrar which "was ascribed to him a century after his unfortunate passage here", no nothing, strictly nothing. Rimbaud is nowhere to be found, absent as ever, and our quest, in confirming what I already knew – Rimbaud eludes us for ever – finds its meaning in the very absence of an outcome. The French Ambassador put up a plaque on an old building in the town, where he imagined that Rimbaud might have stayed, but this gesture brings us no closer to this fragment of life than our vain quest. In fact, perhaps less close; like those who preceded us, we are "in search of a man who fled his past, pursued an impossible future and who, by dint of saying here and now, *leaves no trace*".

It was on this note of effacement that we set off again, casting a parting glance at the view from the barracks: that of the volcano Merbabu, whose basin crater neatly traced out against the sky, seems to spit out plumes of cloud. Perhaps Salatiga possesses the only picture that vaguely recalls the presence of Rimbaud. "The Crater": a quarter of Aden. "You simply can't imagine the place. There's not a tree here, not even a withered one, not a blade of grass, not a patch of earth, not a drop of fresh water. Aden is a volcanic crater . . ." Volcano, fire, lava. "The crater walls prevent the air from getting in, and we're roasting at the bottom of this hole." The places that Rimbaud came to, as it were by chance, swept from one port to the next, become "necessary for the perfection of his suffering", as if in every corner of the world he had to live out the reality of his season in hell. The volcano Merbabu was one of the first circles of hell, while he awaited that of Aden, where he suffered so much.

What does remain of Java in his work is no doubt the fragment of a poem today inscribed on the disputed plaque: "Steeped and peppered lands!" (*"To the steeped and peppered lands! – in the service of the most monstrous industrial and military operations"*, in "Démocratie".)

THE BIRD MARKET

We were about to leave Yogyakarta, once and for all this time, and soon Indonesia. Leaving a world of colours to return to an aseptic reality in grey and white, free of the virus of fantasy – this, at least, is what I felt as I returned to it.

Among the last pictures we were to carry away with us, that of the bird market flung at us pell-mell fragments of Indonesian life. Even when they are poor, even when reduced to the bare necessities of life, the Indonesians consider the possession of a bird essential – in fact not one but several, birds of the wild, with their brilliant plumage and strident cries, straight from the jungles of Sumatra or Irian. From life in the wild, these birds have retained their raucous cries, whether of warning or of threat, a short, sharp sound that penetrates the thick foliage and makes the unwary visitor jump. There is no house, however modest, no palace that does not have its birdcage hung at the front or in the courtyard. After threading our way through a network of lanes with mango and frangipani trees, we emerged in the bird market. We were struck first of all by the sight of these cages, hundreds of them in all shapes and sizes, all in an unbelievable heap. Then the strange creatures that populate them: beside birds, squirrels no bigger than one's thumb to which a girl was feeding banana loaded on a toothpick; scorpions and snakes sharing a stall with a photo of a chuckling baby in the coils of a huge python; giant bats enveloped in their fine membrane and hanging upside down – they are used "for medicine", we were solemnly informed, in particular for asthma, a frequent affliction in this country; a lemur rolled up like a delicate shell, occasionally unrolling this perfect spiral to exhibit huge sad, round eyes; dogs piled into tiny cages and sold for food; a Komodo dragon, more similar to an alligator than to our garden lizards, who was darting out a rapid, forked tongue and whom we were told not to fear (even though on the Komodo Islands, where these prehistoric monsters swarm, all that was found left of a risk-loving photographer was a scrap of his shorts abandoned on the beach); and in the midst of this shambles, huge baskets filled with all kinds of insects, crickets, beetles, grasshoppers, ants in their bark-like skin, a strange seething mass of microscopic life. Looking out over the little huddled monkeys who extended tiny supplicating hands through the bars, a great, arrogant bird of prey eyed the mishmash of insects, tourists and tradesmen.

I know that in Bangkok it is possible, for a few pennies, to open a cage and set a bird free. Not to acquire a bird but to restore it to freedom. For this modest sum we obtain far more than the simple possession of a creature, as those crafty traders, well acquainted as they are with human foibles, understand: we also acquire a sense of our own goodness, or of our vast power, for we are bestowing the greatest gift there is. So, we have the pleasure of the fine deed – doing good – followed by the delectable sight of the bird taking flight; add to that the ever-present possibility of identifying with the captive. In setting the bird free we liberate ourselves as well as everything which, in this world, is wrongly kept behind bars: we become benefactors of humanity, we set things back in proper order, and in addition we take wing along with the bird. Make no mistake, in this act every pleasure is combined, among them the highest to which a person may aspire.

But look what happened to one of our philanthropist friends who had purchased the right to open a good number of cages and see their inhabitants fly away: the birds came back. Almost immediately after leaving the cages they popped back inside, safe from the unknown wilderness. Of course here they found food and security, habits and constraints, restricted and already well-explored boundaries: all that was needed to sustain life, all that, after their test flight, they would not be so reckless as to give up. The fact remains that the birds all rejected the freedom offered them by our generous and idealistic friend. Whether obeying the will of the bird-seller or following their inner compass, they returned one and all to resume life behind bars.

We returned to France to recover, we too, our cherished habits and constraints – having first tried our wings in a little test flight, although, unlike the wise bird, we had acquired a taste for it.

One place is no longer foreign to us. We are no longer looking at the pictures in the travel brochures or postcards seen at a distance, divorced from any living context, obeying no necessity beyond that of creating an effect; now what we have are gestures and actions that we have participated in, because they awaken an echo within us and we understand the need that occasioned them. We are included in these scenes, which are no longer simply spectacle but a sensible reality – a reality sufficiently strong to make us forget our responses and our systems of evaluation. We have entered *their* space, ventured into their country, amazed to discover that it is our own as well. We recognise its existence and the place allotted to it within us, like an area which we have hitherto neglected to explore, one whose extent we have only just grasped. All these unknown possibilities, these unexpressed lives, which the accidents of foreign travel have revealed to us – all that we might have been, done, become . . .

To travel, to leave a particular region in the atlas, but also an inner scene in which one is more or less imprisoned, to step outside of closed mental circuits that have been constructed and cemented into place by habit, to go elsewhere in search of fresh air, to another part of the world and of oneself.

Intake of air, new outlook. Letting go. Inspired by this new freedom, we feel that we could perfectly well stay there, without a backward glance, that in that precise spot and that very moment we are handed the possibility to start anew or to be reborn, to set sail for another land that measures up to our desires – a land far removed from tedium, that grey monster born of a daily round that is inert as an unanswerable truth. We are handed the possibility of entering a country that possesses the promises and consistency of a dream, a dream that we would have been carrying within us all this time while unwittingly neglecting to pursue it. Only an illusion? Possibly, but the important thing is surely to pluck ourselves free of gravity from time to time, to don winged sandals, to push back the horizon bounding us: this is not at all the same thing as *realising* a dream, transforming it into reality – because in that case one would see the end of it – but contriving to inhabit it.

Departure: it is dawn, the horizon opens up, space remains virgin. There would be a look over our shoulder at what has been left behind, and there would be a touch of relief (which would of course need to be tempered with regret). The old adventurer who slumbers deep within us summons us to pack our bags, to set out once more, bundle slung on shoulder, forward march, the world is still in mint condition, there is still time. No matter what follows, we're not talking of a realistic plan, no, of course not, nothing like that, only of the impulse that drives us to set forth, to meet up with our dreams. In Indonesia, storehouse of strong images, powerful detonator of the imagination, I had met one of the possible forms of my own imaginary world. This aspiration towards something different, this picture of the elsewhere, I had been nurturing it for a long time without being able to give it a shape; by a series of slips and slides, it awaited me there, at this far end of the world, more real to me than my previous life.

Or else could it be a disguised form of that violent temptation that sometimes comes over us to be someone else, as in a philosophical study of Balzac, for a few days, a few hours, to borrow someone else's skin, out of simple curiosity, just to try it out, to get away from oneself? The urge to escape, to renewal, a taste of elsewhere – or intolerance of boundaries, or whatever?

Snap the cables, change skin, never mind the metaphor, it always comes down to detachment, to metamorphosis. To leave in order not to return quite to one's starting point.

Once home, a person is no longer the same as he started out, which is why he is never so keen to set off again as at the moment of reaching home. But at the cost of a few strenuous contortions, he picks up his customary yoke, which no longer fits his altered measurements. To step once more back into a role, a character, an attitude: to cut, file, adjust, force a little here and then there, that's it, he has recovered the requisite shape, neither too large nor too small, "the golden mean", and the limits within which he must evolve.

On the plane, returning from Java, I thought that in Paris I would reread Rimbaud; also that I still had some writing to do each morning, confronting my sheet of paper or my computer screen, thus to get back on the road, to relive my departure for Indonesia, to let my imagination reinvent it and look for some extensions – and in this recreated space, to possess it more than at the moment I had lived it: some consolation for having returned . . .

GLOSSARY OF TERMS

abangan: *nominal Muslim whose beliefs owe much to older, pre-Islamic mysticism.*

alun-alun: *main public square of a town or village, usually found in front of the* bupati's *(governor's) residence. Traditionally used for meetings and public ceremonies, they tend nowadays to be deserted, grassy areas.*

Arjuna: *hero of the* Mahabharata *epic.*

ayam: *chicken.*

bajaj: *motorised three wheeler taxi found in Jakarta.*

bale: *Balinese pavilion, house or shelter.*

Bali Aga: *the aboriginal Balinese, who managed to resist the new ways brought in with Majapahit migration.*

barong: *mythical lion-dog creature; star of the* Barong *dance and a firm champion of good in the eternal struggle between good and evil.*

becak: *trishaw (bicycle rickshaw).*

Brahma: *the creator; along with Shiva and Vishnu, one of the trinity of chief Hindu gods.*

brahmana: *scholars and priests, the highest of the four Balinese castes.*

dalang: *storyteller of varied skills and considerable endurance who operates the puppets, tells the story and beats time in a* wayang kulit *shadow puppet performance.*

Galungan: *great Balinese festival, an annual event in the 210 day Balinese* wuku *calendar.*

gamelan: *traditional Javanese and Balinese orchestra, usually almost solely made up of percussion instruments.*

gelandangna: *starving beggars.*

gunung: *mountain.*

halus: *refined, high standards of behaviour and art; characters in* wayang kulit *performances are traditionally either* halus *or* kasar.

kampung: *village, neighbourhood.*

Jubbah: *large white Arab dress, worn by men.*

kafirs: *foreigners, invaders.*

kasar: *rough, coarse, crude; the opposite of* halus.

kraton: *walled city palace; traditional centre of Javanese culture. The two most famous and influential are at Yogyakarta and Solo.*

kris: *wavy-bladed traditional dagger, often held to have spiritual or magical powers.*

lakon: *episode or chapter (for example, in the* Ramayana*).*

lek: *fear, stage fright.*

linga: *male sexual organ.*

Mahabharata: *great Hindu holy book telling of the battle between the Pandavas and the Korawas.*

Majapahit: *last great Hindu dynasty on Java, pushed out of Java into Bali by the rise of Islamic power.*

meru: *multi-roofed shrines in Balinese temples; altar with a pagoda roof for the nature divinities. Their name comes from that of the Hindu holy mountain Mahameruan.*

nasi: *cooked rice.* Nasi goreng *is the ubiquitous fried rice.*

nusa: *island, as in Nusa Penida.*

padmasana: *empty chairs in a temple reserved for the gods.*

priyayi: *the nobility.*

punokawan: *popular characters in the* wayang kulit.

puputan, or puputan raya: *warriors' fight to the death; an honourable but suicidal option when faced with an unbeatable enemy.*

raja: *lord, prince or king.*

Raja seberang: *'the king from overseas'; used to describe white overlords.*

Ramayana: *one of the great Hindu holy books. Stories from the Ramayana form the keystone of many Javanese and Balinese dances and tales.*

Rangda: *witch, black-magic spirit of Balinese tales and dances*

Ratu Adil: *the Just Prince who, according to Javanese legend, will return to liberate Indonesia from oppression.*

santri: *orthodox, devout Muslim.*

sarong (or sarung): *all-purpose cloth, often sewn into a tube and worn by women, men and children.*

sate: *classic Indonesian dish; small pieces of charcoal-grilled meat on a skewer served with spicy peanut sauce.*

satrya lelara: *nomads and beggars searching for enlightenment.*

Shiva: *the destroyer; along with Brahma and Vishnu, one of the trinity of chief Hindu gods.*

sudra: *lowest or common caste, to which most Balinese belong.*

Telek: *dance with white mask.*

Topeng: *wooden mask used in funerary dances.*

trishaw, or bajaj: *a vehicle with three wheels and an engine.*

Vishnu: *the pervader or sustainer.*

waringin: *banyan tree; a large and shady tree with drooping branches. Buddha achieved enlightenment under a banyan tree, and* waringin *are found in many temples in Bali.*

warung: *food stall; a combination corner shop and snack bar.*

wayang golek: *masked dance-drama.*

wayang kulit: *shadow puppet play.*

wesia: *the caste of civil servants.*

yoni: *female sexual organ.*